W9-BLG-379

Better Homes & Gardens®

CHRISTMAS COOKING
FROM THE HEART™

Welcoming the Holidays

Meredith® Consumer Marketing
Des Moines, Iowa

CHRISTMAS COOKING
FROM THE HEART™

MEREDITH CORPORATION CONSUMER MARKETING
Consumer Marketing Product Director: Heather Sorensen
Consumer Marketing Product Manager: Tami Perkins
Consumer Products Marketing Manager: Janece Schwartzkopf
Business Manager: Diane Umland
Senior Production Manager: Al Rodruck

WATERBURY PUBLICATIONS, INC.
Editorial Director: Lisa Kingsley
Creative Director: Ken Carlson
Associate Editor: Tricia Bergman
Associate Design Director: Doug Samuelson
Production Assistant: Mindy Samuelson
Contributing Copy Editor: Peg Smith
Contributing Proofreader: Terri Fredrickson
Contributing Food Stylists: Joshua Hake, Jennifer Peterson

***BETTER HOMES & GARDENS*® MAGAZINE**
Editor in Chief: Stephen Orr
Creative Director: Jennifer D. Madara
Executive Editor: Oma Blaise Ford

MEREDITH CORPORATION
President and CEO: Tom Harty
Executive Chairman: Stephen M. Lacy

In Memoriam: E.T. Meredith III (1933–2003)

Better Homes
& Gardens

TEST KITCHEN

Our seal assures you that every recipe in *Christmas Cooking from the Heart*™ has been tested in the *Better Homes & Gardens*® Test Kitchen. This means that each recipe is practical and reliable and it meets our high standards of taste appeal. We guarantee your satisfaction with this book for as long as you own it.

All of us at Meredith Consumer Marketing are dedicated to providing you with information and ideas to enhance your home. We welcome your comments and suggestions. Write to us at: Meredith Consumer Marketing, 1716 Locust St., Des Moines, IA 50309-3023. *Christmas Cooking from the Heart*™ is available by mail. To order editions from past years, call 800/627-5490.

Cover: Red Velvet Cake
(recipe, page 82)

CHOCOLATE
MIXED NUT PIE,
PAGE 143

SAUSAGE-PESTO
PULL-APART
BREAD, PAGE 35

Table of Contents

Welcoming the Holidays

The holidays can be busy with family get-togethers and gifts to cook or bake for friends and neighbors. And food plays a large roll in embracing the season, remembering celebrations of the past as well as making new memories. *Better Homes & Gardens®* *Christmas Cooking from the Heart™* has recipes you can feel confident about to create a warm and welcoming season for yourself and loved ones. For a hearty brunch, choose Caramel-Banana-Pecan Bread Casserole (page 48) and Spinach-Pancetta Quiche (page 53). For a family feast, try Turkey-Breast Roulade with Sausage and Fennel Stuffing (page 11) and Citrus-Beet Salad (page 27). And what are the holidays without indulgent desserts (Marbleous Chocolate-Peanut Butter Cake with Salted Caramel Glaze, page 85), heavenly breads (Cinnamon Roll Wreath, page 67), and tender cookies (Pistachio Star Sandwiches, page 108, and Snickerdoodle Shortbread page 106). Enjoy these recipes and many more!

Happy Holidays!

KRUMKAKE,
PAGE 114

HERB-AND-GARLIC-
CRUSTED PORK ROAST,
PAGE 11

Memorable Dinner Party

Create a memory-making spread for a crowd or an intimate gathering with these fabulous recipes. From roasts and roulades to gratins, yeast rolls, and salads, these dishes make any meal an event.

TURKEY BREAST
ROULADE WITH
SAUSAGE AND
FENNEL STUFFING

TURKEY BREAST ROULADE WITH SAUSAGE AND FENNEL STUFFING

PREP 45 minutes
COOK 8 minutes
BAKE 35 minutes at 375°F
STAND 15 minutes

8   oz. bulk Italian sausage
¼   cup chopped onion
¼   cup chopped celery
1   clove garlic, minced
¼   cup dry white wine
1   tsp. fennel seeds, crushed
¼   tsp. ground nutmeg
¾   cup Italian seasoned fine dry bread crumbs
2   1½- to 2-lb. boneless turkey breast halves
1   Tbsp. butter, melted
     Salt and black pepper

1. For stuffing, in a large skillet cook the sausage, onion, and celery over medium-high heat, stirring frequently, until sausage is browned and vegetables are tender. Add garlic and cook 2 minutes more. Remove from heat and stir in wine, fennel seeds, and nutmeg. Stir in bread crumbs. Set aside to cool.
2. Preheat oven to 375°F. Place a turkey breast half on a cutting board, skin side down. With a knife parallel to the cutting board, cut turkey in half to, but not through, the other side. Open like a book. Repeat with the second breast half. Place one breast half between two sheets of plastic wrap. With a meat mallet or rolling pin, pound meat to a uniform ½-inch thickness. Repeat with remaining breast half. Remove plastic wrap; spread half the stuffing onto each turkey breast half, leaving a border around edges. Roll up turkey breast, starting with the long end, ending with the skin on top. Secure at 2-inch intervals with 100%-cotton kitchen string. Brush rolls with melted butter. Sprinkle with salt and pepper. Place rolls on a rack in a shallow baking pan.
3. Roast 35 to 45 minutes or until an instant-read thermometer inserted in center registers 165°F. Remove from oven, tent loosely with foil; let stand 15 minutes. Remove twine. Cut into slices. Makes 8 servings.
PER SERVING *351 cal., 12 g fat (5 g sat. fat), 131 mg chol., 535 mg sodium, 9 g carb., 1 g fiber, 1 g sugars, 48 g pro.*

HERB-AND-GARLIC-CRUSTED PORK ROAST
(PICTURED ON PAGE 8)

PREP 25 minutes
BRINE 8 hours
ROAST 15 minutes at 425°F
BAKE 45 minutes at 350°F
STAND 15 minutes

8   cups cold water
½   cup kosher salt
¼   cup brown sugar
1   center cut, natural* boneless pork loin, approximately 3 to 3½ lb.
1½   cups fresh bread crumbs
3   Tbsp. peanut or vegetable oil
4   slices Black Forest bacon or other thick-sliced bacon, cut in 1-inch pieces (uncooked)
1   Tbsp. apricot preserves
2   tsp. finely chopped fresh garlic
3   tsp. chopped fresh rosemary
3   Tbsp. chopped fresh parsley
½   tsp. freshly ground black pepper
½   tsp. kosher salt
3   Tbsp. butter, melted

1. For brine, in an extra-large bowl dissolve salt and sugar in 8 cups cold water. Transfer pork to brine; make sure it is fully submerged. Cover; refrigerate overnight.
2. Spread bread crumbs on a baking sheet. Let stand overnight to dry.**
3. Remove loin from brine; pat dry with paper towels. Heat oil in a nonstick skillet. Add pork and brown on all sides, about 10 minutes. Let cool slightly.
4. In a food processor puree uncooked bacon to a smooth paste.*** Transfer half to a bowl. Stir in apricot preserves, garlic, and 2 teaspoons of the rosemary.
5. Position oven rack in lowest position. Preheat oven to 425°F. Place pork on waxed paper. Spread with bacon mixture. In another bowl combine the bread crumbs, parsley, remaining rosemary, pepper, ½ teaspoon kosher salt, and the melted butter. Toss to combine. Evenly press a layer of crumb mixture on the roast (except ends), applying enough pressure for crumbs to adhere to bacon layer.
6. Transfer roast to a wire rack in a foil-lined baking pan or roasting pan. Roast 15 minutes. Reduce oven temperature to 350°F. Roast 45 minutes more or until an instant-read thermometer registers 145°F. (If crust begins to brown too much, tent roast with foil.) Remove roast from oven;

tent with foil. Let rest 15 minutes. Makes 8 servings.
* If you are not able to find a natural pork roast that does not have water added, skip the brining step.
** Or spread fresh bread crumbs in a 15×10-inch baking pan. Bake at 300°F 10 minutes or until dry, stirring once or twice. Crumbs will continue to dry as they cool.
*** This amount of bacon is necessary for the processor blades to work. Use the remaining puree to make this easy appetizer: Spread on baguette slices then broil until golden. Serve with fruit chutney.
PER SERVING *412 cal., 23 fat (8 g sat. fat), 118 mg chol., 621 mg sodium, 13 g carb., 1 g fiber, 2 g sugars, 36 g pro.*

CRANBERRY-FIG RELISH

PREP 10 minutes
CHILL 2 hours

½   cup dried figs, stems removed
2   cups fresh or frozen* cranberries
1   Tbsp. snipped fresh mint leaves (optional)
½   cup orange marmalade
1   Tbsp. balsamic vinegar

1. Place figs in a food processor. Cover and pulse to large pieces. Add cranberries and pulse until mixture is coarsely chopped. Transfer to a medium bowl; if desired, add mint.
2. In a small bowl stir together marmalade and vinegar. Add to cranberry mixture; mix well. Cover and chill at least 2 hours. Makes 2 cups.
* If using frozen cranberries, measure while frozen. Let stand at room temperature about 15 minutes to thaw slightly before processing.
Make Ahead Prepare as directed. Place in an airtight container. Seal; chill up to 3 days. Or label and freeze up to 6 months. Thaw overnight in the refrigerator.
PER SERVING *88 cal., 0 fat, 0 mg chol., 13 mg sodium, 23 g carb., 2 g fiber, 18 g sugars, 0 g pro.*

COFFEE-BRAISED POT ROAST

COFFEE-BRAISED POT ROAST

PREP 30 minutes
BAKE 2 hours 30 minutes at 325°F
COOK 10 minutes

1	3- to 3½-lb. beef chuck pot roast, trimmed of fat
1	tsp. salt
½	tsp. black pepper
1	Tbsp. vegetable oil
1	large onion, halved and sliced
1	medium green sweet pepper, cut into 2-inch pieces
3	cloves garlic, minced
¾	cup beef broth
1	8-oz. can crushed pineapple (juice pack), undrained
1	Tbsp. instant espresso or French roast coffee powder
¼	tsp. crushed red pepper
¼	tsp. ground allspice
2	lb. sweet potatoes, peeled, halved lengthwise, and cut into 2-inch pieces
	Coarsely chopped parsley (optional)

1. Preheat oven to 325°F. Sprinkle meat with salt and black pepper. In a 6-quart Dutch oven heat oil over medium-high heat. Add meat; brown meat on all sides. Remove from pot.

2. Add onion, sweet pepper, and garlic to Dutch oven. Cook and stir 4 to 5 minutes or until onion and garlic are tender and starting to brown. Return meat to Dutch oven. Add next five ingredients (through allspice). Bring to boiling. Cover pot and transfer to oven.

3. Roast 1¾ hours. Add sweet potatoes. Cover and roast 45 minutes more or until meat and vegetables are tender. Transfer to a platter; cover to keep warm.

4. For sauce, bring cooking liquid to boiling; reduce heat. Simmer, uncovered, 10 to 15 minutes or until slightly thickened. Serve pot roast with sauce. If desired, sprinkle with parsley and additional crushed red pepper. Makes 8 servings.

PER SERVING *345 cal., 9 g fat (3 g sat. fat), 111 mg chol., 539 mg sodium, 24 g carb., 3 g fiber, 9 g sugars, 40 g pro.*

SESAME-CRUSTED ROAST CHICKEN

PREP 20 minutes
ROAST 1 hour 15 minutes at 425°F
STAND 5 minutes

- ⅓ cup reduced-sodium soy sauce or tamari sauce
- 2 Tbsp. toasted sesame oil
- 2 Tbsp. sesame seeds
- 1 Tbsp. grated fresh ginger
- 4 cloves garlic, minced
- 1 tsp. freshly cracked black pepper
- 1 3½- to 4-lb. whole chicken
- ¼ tsp. salt
- 1 lb. small new yellow or red potatoes, scrubbed and halved
- ⅓ cup reduced-sodium chicken broth (optional)
- 2 Tbsp. coarsely chopped parsley

1. Preheat oven to 425°F. In a small bowl whisk together soy sauce, 1 tablespoon of sesame oil, and the next four ingredients (through pepper). Pat chicken dry; season with salt. Fold legs up over breast. Tie legs together with 100%-cotton kitchen string. Twist wing tips under back.

2. Heat a 12-inch cast-iron skillet over medium-high heat until very hot, 3 to 5 minutes. Add remaining sesame oil to skillet; heat 30 seconds. Place chicken, breast side down, in skillet. Sear 3 minutes or until golden and crusty. Turn chicken and sear 3 minutes. Remove skillet from heat.

3. Scatter potatoes around chicken. Pour the soy sauce mixture over chicken and potatoes. Roast 1¼ to 1½ hours or until a thermometer inserted in thighs registers 170°F, stirring potatoes and spooning skillet drippings over chicken once or twice during cooking. If sauce evaporates during roasting, add broth. Remove skillet from oven. Cover chicken; let rest 5 minutes. Sprinkle potatoes with parsley before serving. Makes 6 servings.
PER SERVING *503 cal., 32 g fat (8 g sat. fat), 134 mg chol., 652 mg sodium, 15 g carb., 2 g fiber, 3 g sugars, 36 g pro.*

CHIVE-DILL DINNER ROLLS

PREP 35 minutes
SLOW COOK 2 hours (high)
BROIL 3 minutes

Nonstick cooking spray
1   Tbsp. yellow cornmeal
3   to 3¼ cups all-purpose flour
1   pkg. active dry yeast
1½ tsp. salt
¼   cup snipped fresh chives or thinly
     sliced green onions
2   to 3 Tbsp. snipped fresh dill or 1 tsp.
     dried dill
1¼ cups warm water (120°F to 130°F)
5   Tbsp. butter, melted
½   cup yellow cornmeal

1. Line a 5- to 6-quart oval slow cooker with parchment paper. Coat with cooking spray and sprinkle with 1 tablespoon cornmeal.
2. In a large bowl stir together 1½ cups of the flour, the yeast, salt, chives, and dill. Add the warm water and 4 tablespoons of the melted butter. Beat with a mixer on medium 30 seconds, scraping bowl as needed. Beat on high 3 minutes. Stir in ½ cup cornmeal and as much of the remaining flour as you can.
3. Turn dough out onto a lightly floured surface. Knead in enough remaining flour to make a moderately stiff dough that is smooth and elastic (6 to 8 minutes). Shape dough into 16 balls by pulling dough and pinching underneath. Place balls in prepared cooker (sides will touch).
4. Cover and cook on high 2 to 2½ hours or until an instant-read thermometer registers 195°F (tops of rolls may be slightly wet). Use parchment paper to transfer rolls to a wire rack.
5. Place an oven rack 4 to 5 inches from the broiler. Preheat broiler. Place rolls (without parchment paper) on a baking sheet. Brush tops with remaining 1 tablespoon melted butter. Broil 3 to 4 minutes or until lightly browned. Sprinkle with additional dill. Makes 16 servings.
PER SERVING *137 cal., 4 g fat (2 g sat. fat), 10 mg chol., 248 mg sodium, 22 g carb., 1 g fiber, 0 g sugars, 3 g pro.*

BAKED RISOTTO WITH PORTOBELLO MUSHROOMS

PREP 15 minutes
BAKE 35 minutes at 350°F

Nonstick cooking spray
6   oz. fresh portobello mushroom
     caps, halved and sliced (2½ cups)
½   cup chopped onion
1   to 2 cloves garlic, minced
2   tsp. olive oil
2   14.5-oz. cans reduced-sodium
     chicken broth
1   cup water
1½ cups uncooked Arborio rice
½   tsp. freshly ground black pepper
1½ cups chopped cooked chicken
     breast, warmed
½   cup grated Parmesan cheese
2   Tbsp. snipped fresh parsley

1. Preheat oven to 350°F. Coat a 2-quart baking dish with cooking spray. In a large skillet cook mushrooms, onion, and garlic in hot oil over medium heat until mushrooms are tender, stirring occasionally.
2. Add broth and the water; bring to boiling. Stir in rice and pepper. Transfer to prepared baking dish. Bake, covered, 35 minutes or until rice is tender.
3. Stir in chicken, cheese, and parsley. Top with additional parsley. Makes 6 servings.
PER SERVING *234 cal., 5 g fat (2 g sat. fat), 35 mg chol., 468 mg sodium, 30 g carb., 1 g fiber, 2 g sugars, 18 g pro.*

ROMESCO SAUCE

START TO FINISH 20 minutes

4   medium roma tomatoes, peeled,
     seeded, and cut up
⅔   cup bottled roasted red sweet
     peppers, cut up
1   ¾-inch slice country-style bread,
     toasted and torn into pieces (2 oz.)
½   cup blanched whole almonds,
     toasted (see tip, page 49)
¼   cup sherry vinegar or red wine
     vinegar
4   cloves garlic, smashed
1   Tbsp. snipped fresh parsley
1   tsp. smoked paprika
½   tsp. ground ancho chile pepper
⅛   tsp. cayenne pepper
¼   to ⅓ cup olive oil
     Salt

1. In a food processor combine the first 10 ingredients (through cayenne pepper). Cover and process until combined. With the motor running, add oil through the feed tube in a thin steady stream until mixture is finely chopped. Season to taste with salt. Serve over meat, poultry, or fish.
2. Refrigerate leftovers, covered, up to 1 week. Before serving, let stand 30 minutes at room temperature. Makes 16 servings.
PER SERVING *76 cal., 6 g fat (1 g sat. fat), 0 mg chol., 61 mg sodium, 5 g carb., 1 g fiber, 1 g sugars, 2 g pro.*

CHIVE-DILL
DINNER ROLLS

CARAWAY-RYE
BEER BREAD

CARAWAY-RYE BEER BREAD

PREP 15 minutes
SLOW COOK 2½ hours (high)
COOL 10 minutes

    Nonstick cooking spray
1½ cups all-purpose flour
½   cup rye flour
½   cup regular rolled oats
1   Tbsp. sugar
1   Tbsp. baking powder
1   tsp. salt
2   tsp. caraway seeds
½   tsp. baking soda
1   12-oz. bottle or can Lager, pilsner,
    or wheat beer
    Coarse salt
    Dijon mustard (optional)

1. Coat a 3½- or 4-quart oval slow cooker with cooking spray. In a large bowl stir together next eight ingredients (through baking soda).
2. Add beer all at once to flour mixture; stir just until combined (batter will be sticky). Spoon into prepared cooker; smooth top. Sprinkle with additional oats and/or coarse salt.
3. Cover and cook on high 2½ hours or until a toothpick comes out clean, giving crockery liner a half-turn halfway through, if possible.
4. Turn off cooker. If possible, remove crockery liner from cooker. Carefully remove lid so condensation does not drip onto bread. Cover opening completely with paper towels; replace lid. Cool 10 minutes. Remove bread; cool completely on a wire rack. If desired, serve with mustard. Makes 12 servings.
PER SERVING *123 cal., 1 g fat (0 g sat. fat), 0 mg chol., 393 mg sodium, 24 g carb., 2 g fiber, 1 g sugars, 4 g pro.*

TOASTED MILLET NO-KNEAD WHOLE WHEAT ROLLS

PREP 25 minutes
RISE 1 hour 15 minutes
ROAST 25 minutes at 400°F
COOL 10 minutes

2   cups whole wheat flour
5   Tbsp. yellow cornmeal
2   pkg. active dry yeast
1½ tsp. salt
½   cup millet
2   cups milk

TOASTED MILLET NO-KNEAD WHOLE WHEAT ROLLS

⅓   cup butter, cut up
2   eggs
3   Tbsp. molasses
2   to 2½ cups all-purpose flour
2   Tbsp. butter, melted

1. In a large bowl stir together whole wheat flour, 4 tablespoons of the cornmeal, yeast, and salt.
2. In a large saucepan cook millet over medium heat 5 minutes or until toasted with a nutty aroma, stirring occasionally. Add milk and ⅓ cup butter. Heat and stir just until warm (120°F to 130°F) and butter is almost melted. Add milk mixture to yeast mixture; add eggs and molasses. Beat with a mixer on low 30 seconds, scraping bowl constantly. Beat on high 3 minutes. Stir in as much of the all-purpose flour as you can to make a soft, yet firm dough.

3. Cover and let rise in a warm place until double in size (45 to 60 minutes).
4. Lightly grease a 13×9-inch baking pan. Punch dough down; turn out onto a floured surface. Using floured hands, press dough into an 11×7-inch rectangle. Cut into 24 pieces; transfer to prepared pan. Cover and let rise in a warm place until double in size (30 to 40 minutes).
5. Preheat oven to 400°F. Brush rolls with melted butter and sprinkle with remaining 1 tablespoon cornmeal. Bake 25 minutes or until rolls are golden and sound hollow when lightly tapped. Cool in pan 10 minutes. Serve warm. Makes 24 servings.
PER SERVING *151 cal., 5 g fat (3 g sat. fat), 26 mg chol., 191 mg sodium, 23 g carb., 2 g fiber, 3 g sugars, 4 g pro.*

CABBAGE AND POTATO GRATIN

CABBAGE AND POTATO GRATIN

PREP 20 minutes
ROAST 1 hour at 425°F

2   Tbsp. butter, softened
1½ lb. Yukon gold potatoes, thinly sliced
1   medium head cabbage, cored and shredded
½   cup shredded Gruyère
1½ cups heavy cream
2   Tbsp. chopped fresh thyme
3   cloves garlic, minced
1½ tsp. salt
½   cup panko bread crumbs
1   Tbsp. olive oil

1. Preheat oven to 425°F. Butter a 3-quart baking dish. In two layers add Yukon gold potatoes, cabbage, and Gruyère. In a bowl combine cream, thyme, garlic, and salt; pour over cabbage.
2. Bake, covered, 30 minutes. Uncover; bake 15 minutes more. In a small bowl mix together panko and oil. Sprinkle over gratin. Bake 15 minutes or until golden brown. Makes 8 servings.
PER SERVING *312 cal., 23 g fat (14 g sat. fat), 66 mg chol., 485 mg sodium, 21 g carb., 3 g fiber, 4 g sugars, 6 g pro.*

CELERY ROOT PUREE

START TO FINISH 30 minutes

3   lb. celery root, peeled and cut into ½-inch cubes (8 cups)
4   small cloves garlic, peeled
2   tsp. kosher salt
1   cup heavy cream
½   cup unsalted butter
     Black pepper
     Celery root leaves (optional)

1. In a large saucepan combine celery root, garlic, and kosher salt. Add enough water to cover. Bring to boiling. Reduce heat; simmer, covered, 12 to 15 minutes or until tender; drain. Transfer to a food processor.
2. Puree mixture with the cream and butter until smooth. Season to taste with pepper and additional salt. If desired, top with additional butter and celery root leaves before serving. Makes 8 servings.
PER SERVING *277 cal., 23 g fat (14 g sat. fat), 64 mg chol., 672 mg sodium, 17 g carb., 3 g fiber, 4 g sugars, 4 g pro.*

CELERY ROOT PUREE

ROASTED SMASHED POTATOES

PREP 20 minutes
COOK 25 minutes
COOL 10 minutes
ROAST 22 minutes at 450°F

12   to 16 small red potatoes (1½ to 2 inches in diameter)
1¾   tsp. salt
¼   cup olive oil
½   tsp. black pepper
¾   cup finely shredded Parmesan cheese (3 oz.)
2   Tbsp. finely snipped fresh Italian parsley

1. In a large covered saucepan cook potatoes with 1 teaspoon of the salt in enough boiling water to cover 25 to 30 minutes or until very tender; drain.
2. Preheat oven to 450°F. Line a 15×10-inch baking pan with foil. Transfer potatoes to prepared pan; cool 10 minutes. Using a potato masher or the palm of your hand, lightly smash each potato to ½-inch thickness, keeping potato in one piece. Brush with half the oil and sprinkle with ½ teaspoon of the salt and ¼ teaspoon of the pepper.
3. Roast 10 to 15 minutes or until bottoms are light brown and crisp. Turn potatoes; brush with remaining oil and sprinkle with remaining salt and pepper. Roast 10 to 15 minutes more or until potatoes are light brown and crisp. In a small bowl combine cheese and parsley; sprinkle over potatoes. Roast 2 to 3 minutes or until cheese is melted. Makes 6 servings.
PER SERVING *202 cal., 12 g fat (2 g sat. fat), 8 mg chol., 514 mg sodium, 18 g carb., 2 g fiber, 2 g sugars, 6 g pro.*

ROASTED
SMASHED
POTATOES

FRENCH ONION SOUP

FRENCH ONION SOUP

START TO FINISH 30 minutes

2   Tbsp. butter
2   cups thinly sliced yellow onions
1   32-oz. box reduced-sodium beef
    broth
2   Tbsp. dry sherry or dry white wine
    (optional)
1   tsp. Worcestershire sauce
    Dash black pepper
4   slices French or Italian bread,
    toasted*
¾   cup shredded Swiss, Gruyère, or
    Jarlsberg cheese (3 oz.)
    Dried thyme (optional)
    Chopped chives (optional)

1. In a large saucepan melt butter; add onions. Cook, covered, over medium-low heat 8 to 10 minutes or until tender and golden, stirring occasionally.
2. Add broth, sherry (if using), Worcestershire sauce, and pepper to onions in saucepan. Bring to boiling; reduce heat. Simmer, covered, 10 minutes.
3. Meanwhile, place an oven rack 3 to 4 inches from broiler. Preheat broiler. Arrange toasted bread on a foil-lined baking sheet; sprinkle with cheese. Broil 1 minute or until cheese is melted and is lightly browned. If desired, sprinkle bread with thyme. Top soup with toasted bread and sprinkle with chives, if desired. Makes 4 servings.
***** To toast bread, place slices on a baking sheet. Bake at 350°F 7 to 10 minutes or until golden brown, turning once halfway. Or broil slices 2 minutes on each side.
PER SERVING *251 cal., 13 g fat (8 g sat. fat), 35 mg chol., 776 mg sodium, 22 g carb., 2 g fiber, 5 g sugars, 12 g pro.*

NEW ENGLAND CLAM CHOWDER

START TO FINISH 30 minutes

1   pint shucked clams or two 6.5-oz.
    cans minced clams, undrained
1   8-oz. bottle clam juice
3   slices bacon, chopped
1   cup chopped onion
½   cup chopped celery
3   cups chopped, peeled potatoes
1   tsp. snipped fresh thyme
¼   tsp. black pepper
2   cups half-and-half

NEW ENGLAND CLAM CHOWDER

1. Chop fresh clams (if using), reserving juice; set clams aside. Strain fresh clam juice to remove bits of shell. (Or drain canned clams, reserving juice.) Add enough bottled clam juice to reserved clam juice to measure 2 cups.
2. In a 3-quart pot cook bacon over medium heat until crisp. Drain bacon on paper towels, reserving 1 tablespoon drippings in pot. Add onion and celery to reserved drippings. Cook 5 minutes or until soft, stirring occasionally.
3. Add the 2 cups clam juice, potatoes, thyme, and pepper. Bring to boiling; reduce heat. Simmer 10 to 15 minutes or until potatoes are tender. Using a slotted spoon, remove 1 cup potatoes; set aside. Using a handheld immersion blender, blend soup until smooth.*
4. Add clams and reserved potatoes to soup. Return to boiling; reduce heat and cook 1 minute. Stir in half-and-half; heat through. Sprinkle servings with bacon and, if desired, additional thyme. Makes 6 servings.
***Tip** Or transfer soup, one-fourth at a time, to a blender or food processor. Cover and blend until smooth. Return to pot.
PER SERVING *278 cal., 14 g fat (7 g sat. fat), 58 mg chol., 633 mg sodium, 22 g carb., 2 g fiber, 5 g sugars, 17 g pro.*

LEMON TOASTED FARRO AND CAULIFLOWER PILAF

PREP 30 minutes
COOK 43 minutes

1	Tbsp. olive oil
1½	cups farro
3	cups water
½	cup chopped onion
½	tsp. salt
1	lemon
2	cups small cauliflower florets
3	cloves garlic, minced
1½	tsp. ground turmeric
¼	tsp. black pepper
1	Tbsp. snipped fresh thyme

1. In a large heavy saucepan heat oil over medium-high. Add farro; cook and stir 5 to 6 minutes or until farro is toasted and has a nutty aroma. Stir in the water, onion, and salt. Bring to boiling; reduce heat. Simmer, covered, about 30 minutes or just until farro is tender.

2. Remove 2 teaspoons zest and squeeze 3 tablespoons juice from lemon. Stir lemon zest, cauliflower, garlic, turmeric, and pepper into farro mixture.

3. Cook, covered, over medium-high heat 4 minutes. Uncover; cook 4 minutes more or until cauliflower is tender and liquid is absorbed, stirring occasionally. Stir in lemon juice and thyme. Makes 10 servings.

PER SERVING *126 cal., 2 g fat (0 g sat. fat), 0 mg chol., 125 mg sodium, 23 g carb., 4 g fiber, 1 g sugars, 4 g pro.*

WINTER BULGUR SALAD WITH OLIVE DRESSING

START TO FINISH 25 minutes

1	cup bulgur
2	cups boiling water
2	cups chopped cauliflower
½	cup pitted kalamata and/or green olives, coarsely chopped
3	Tbsp. fresh lemon juice
3	Tbsp. olive oil
1	clove garlic, minced
	Freshly ground black pepper
4	oz. feta cheese, crumbled
4	cups torn chicories, such as escarole, radicchio, and/or endive
6	celery stalks, thinly bias sliced

1. Place bulgur in a large heat-proof bowl. Pour the boiling water over bulgur; cover. Let stand 15 minutes.

2. Meanwhile, place cauliflower in a food processor. Pulse three to five times, just until finely chopped.

3. For olive D\dressing, in a small bowl stir together olives, lemon juice, olive oil, and garlic. Season with black pepper to taste.

4. Drain bulgur; return to bowl. Stir in cauliflower, olives, and feta. Arrange bulgur mixture, chicories, and celery, on a platter. Drizzle with olive dressing. Makes 4 servings.

PER SERVING *361 cal., 21 g fat (6 g sat. fat), 25 mg chol., 744 mg sodium, 35 g carb., 8 g fiber, 3 g sugars, 10 g pro.*

LEMON TOASTED
FARRO AND
CAULIFLOWER PILAF

**ROASTED CABBAGE
WITH OLIVE
TAPENADE**

ROASTED CABBAGE WITH OLIVE TAPENADE

PREP 15 minutes
ROAST 35 minutes at 425°F

2   1¼- to 1¾- lb. heads red and/or
    green cabbage, trimmed and
    cut lengthwise into 1-inch slices
    (discard cores)
1   shallot, halved and sliced
4   cloves garlic, minced
½   tsp. kosher salt
¼   tsp. freshly ground black pepper
¼   cup olive oil
¼   cup pesto or olive tapenade

1. Preheat oven to 425°F. Place cabbage
in a 15×10-inch baking pan, overlapping
slightly if necessary. Sprinkle with shallot,
garlic, salt, and pepper; drizzle with oil.
2. Roast 35 to 40 minutes or until
cabbage is tender, turning once halfway
through and spreading with pesto. Makes
8 servings.
PER SERVING 107 cal., 7 g fat (1 g sat. fat),
0 mg chol., 206 mg sodium, 10 g carb.,
4 g fiber, 5 g sugars, 2 g pro.

ROASTED ONIONS AND FENNEL WITH PROSCIUTTO

PREP 20 minutes
ROAST 35 minutes at 400°F

3   medium fennel bulbs, trimmed and
    cut into 1-inch wedges
2   medium red onions, cut into 1-inch
    wedges
2   Tbsp. olive oil
¼   tsp. salt
¼   tsp. black pepper
2   oz. prosciutto, cut into shreds
2   Tbsp. finely shredded Asiago
    cheese
1   tsp. snipped fresh thyme
    Snipped fennel fronds

1. Preheat oven to 400°F. In a shallow
baking pan combine fennel wedges and
onions. Drizzle with oil and sprinkle with
salt and pepper; toss to coat.
2. Roast 35 to 40 minutes or until tender
and lightly browned, stirring occasionally.
Sprinkle with prosciutto, cheese, thyme,
and fennel fronds. Makes 6 servings.
PER SERVING 132 cal., 8 g fat (1 g sat. fat),
3 mg chol., 353 mg sodium, 12 g carb.,
4 g fiber, 2 g sugars, 5 g pro.

ROASTED ONIONS
AND FENNEL WITH
PROSCIUTTO

CITRUS-BEET
SALAD

CITRUS-BEET SALAD

PREP 25 minutes
COOK 40 minutes
CHILL 2 hours
STAND 30 minutes

6   medium beets (about 24 oz.)
2   oranges
6   Tbsp. walnut oil or canola oil
2   Tbsp. white wine vinegar or white vinegar
6   Tbsp. crumbled feta cheese
¼   cup broken walnuts, toasted (tip, page 49)
5   kumquats, sliced
½   tsp. coarsely ground black pepper

1. Cut off all but 1 inch of the stems and roots of beets. Wash beets; do not peel. In a large saucepan cook beets, covered, in boiling salted water 40 to 50 minutes or until tender. Drain; cool slightly. Slip skins off beets; discard skins. Cut beets into chunks; place in a medium bowl.

2. Meanwhile, for dressing, remove 2 teaspoons zest and squeeze ¼ cup juice from one of the oranges; place in a screw-top jar. Add oil and vinegar. Cover and shake well. Drizzle half the dressing over cooked beets; toss gently to coat. Cover and chill at least 2 hours or up to 24 hours.

3. Let salad stand at room temperature 30 minutes. Peel and slice the remaining orange; add to beets. Sprinkle salad with feta cheese, nuts, kumquats, and pepper. Drizzle with remaining dressing. Serve with a slotted spoon. Makes 8 servings.

PER SERVING *149 cal., 14 g fat (2 g sat. fat), 4 mg chol., 83 mg sodium, 6 g carb., 2 g fiber, 0 g sugars, 2 g pro.*

ORANGE-BRAISED CARROTS WITH RAISINS

START TO FINISH 30 minutes

1   lb. small or medium carrots, scrubbed, peeled (if desired), and halved if large
¾   cup fresh orange juice
⅓   cup golden raisins
1   3-inch cinnamon stick
1   Tbsp. unsalted butter
½   tsp. salt
1   Tbsp. chopped fresh dill weed
    Freshly ground black pepper

**ORANGE-BRAISED
CARROTS WITH
RAISINS**

1. In a large skillet combine the first six ingredients (through salt.) Add ½ cup water. Bring to boiling over high heat; reduce to medium. Cook 15 minutes or until almost all liquid has evaporated and carrots are glazed and just tender, turning carrots occasionally. Discard cinnamon stick.

2. Transfer carrots and raisins to a platter. Top with dill. Sprinkle with freshly ground black pepper. Makes 4 servings.

PER SERVING *135 cal., 3 g fat (2 g sat. fat), 8 mg chol., 321 mg sodium, 27 g carb., 4 g fiber, 17 g sugars, 2 g pro.*

KALE–WHITE CHEDDAR
GALETTE, PAGE 35

Spot-On Appetizers

Serve a few of these savory starters and holiday drinks as a prelude to dinner or feature a collection as an appetizer buffet. Either way, there's something for everyone to enjoy.

VIETNAMESE PORK
MEATBALLS

VIETNAMESE PORK MEATBALLS

START TO FINISH 35 minutes

1¼ lb. ground pork
4 tsp. grated fresh ginger
1 Tbsp. smashed and finely chopped fresh lemongrass
2 tsp. fish sauce
1½ tsp. lime zest
1 clove garlic, minced
1 Tbsp. canola oil
 Thinly sliced cabbage, shredded carrots, thinly sliced radishes, fresh cilantro sprigs, and/or lime wedges (optional)

1. In a large bowl combine first six ingredients (through garlic). Shape mixture into twenty 1½-inch meatballs.
2. In an extra-large skillet heat oil over medium-high heat. Add meatballs; cook 12 to 15 minutes or until done (165°F), turning occasionally.
3. If desired, serve meatballs with cabbage, carrots, radishes, cilantro, and/or lime wedges. Makes 4 servings.
PER SERVING *344 cal., 26 g fat (7 g sat. fat), 96 mg chol., 332 mg sodium, 2 g carb., 0 g fiber, 0 g sugars, 26 g pro.*

BUFFALO WINGS WITH BLUE CHEESE DIP

PREP 30 minutes
SLOW COOK 4 hours (low) or 2 hours (high)

16 chicken wings (about 3 lb.)
1½ cups bottled chili sauce
3 to 4 Tbsp. bottled hot pepper sauce
1 recipe Blue Cheese Dip or bottled ranch salad dressing

1. Cut off and discard wing tips. Cut each wing into two sections. Place chicken on the unheated rack of a broiler pan. Broil 4 to 5 inches from heat 10 minutes or until chicken is browned, turning once. Transfer to a 3½- or 4-quart slow cooker. Combine chili sauce and hot pepper sauce; pour over chicken wings.
2. Cover and cook on low 4 to 5 hours or high 2 to 2½ hours. Serve chicken wings with Blue Cheese Dip or ranch salad dressing. Makes 16 servings.
PER SERVING *108 cal., 8 g fat (3 g sat. fat), 21 mg chol., 217 mg sodium, 3 g carb., 0 g fiber, 0 g sugars, 6 g pro.*

BUFFALO WINGS WITH BLUE CHEESE DIP

Blue Cheese Dip In a blender combine one 8-ounce container sour cream; ½ cup mayonnaise or salad dressing; ½ cup crumbled blue cheese (2 oz.); 1 clove garlic, minced; and 1 tablespoon white wine vinegar or white vinegar. Cover and blend until smooth. Store dip, covered, in the refrigerator up to 2 weeks. If desired, sprinkle with additional crumbled blue cheese just before serving.

TURKEY-SAGE SPANAKOPITA

PREP 35 minutes
ROAST 25 minutes at 450°F/15 minutes at 400°F
COOK 6 minutes

1   lb. butternut squash, peeled, seeded, and cut into 1-inch cubes
2   Tbsp. plus 1 tsp. olive oil
½   tsp. salt
½   cup chopped onion
2   cloves garlic, minced
⅓   cup heavy cream
12   oz. Swiss chard, stemmed and coarsely chopped
1½   cups chopped cooked turkey
½   cup crumbled blue cheese
2   Tbsp. chopped fresh sage
5   sheets frozen phyllo dough (14×9-inch rectangles), thawed
2   Tbsp. butter, melted
      Fresh sage leaves

1. Preheat oven to 450°F. Line a baking pan with foil. Combine squash, 1 tablespoon of the oil, and the salt in pan. Toss to coat. Roast, uncovered, 25 to 30 minutes or until tender, stirring occasionally. Remove; let cool. Reduce oven to 400°F.
2. Meanwhile, in an 8- to 9-inch cast-iron skillet* heat 2 teaspoons of the oil over medium-high. Add onion and garlic; cook and stir 3 to 4 minutes or until onion is tender. Stir in cream; bring to boiling. Remove from heat.
3. In a Dutch oven heat remaining 2 teaspoons of the oil over medium-high heat. Add chard; cook and stir 3 minutes or just until wilted. Drain chard in a colander, pressing gently to remove excess liquid. Return chard to Dutch oven. Stir in squash, turkey, cheese, and chopped sage. Add chard mixture to onion mixture in skillet; stir to combine.
4. Unfold phyllo dough; remove one sheet. (Keep remaining phyllo covered with plastic wrap to prevent it from drying out.) Brush phyllo with some of the melted butter. Fold in half to make a 7×9-inch rectangle. Place on top of chard mixture in skillet. Repeat with remaining phyllo, brushing lightly with butter between folded sheets and rotating slightly to stagger corners. (Sheets may tear a little.) Brush with remaining butter. Using a sharp knife, cut a few slits in phyllo.
5. Bake 15 minutes or until top is golden. Sprinkle with sage leaves. Makes 4 servings.
* If you don't have an 8- or 9-inch cast-iron skillet, use a 1½-quart casserole dish. Use the Dutch oven to cook the onion and garlic mixture in Step 2; remove and set aside. Cook chard mixture as in Step 3. Add onion mixture to turkey mixture. Transfer to the casserole dish. Continue with Step 4, layering the phyllo over the mixture in the casserole dish.
PER SERVING 436 cal, 28 g fat (13 g sat. fat), 102 mg chol., 486 mg sodium, 27 g carb., 4 g fiber, 5 g sugars, 23 g pro.

CARIBBEAN COCKTAIL SAUSAGES

PREP 10 minutes
SLOW COOK 4 hours (low)

1   lime
1   12-oz. jar apricot preserves or tropical fruit preserves
2   cloves garlic, minced
1   tsp. Jamaican jerk seasoning
1   tsp. ground ginger
      Few dashes bottled hot pepper sauce
1   14 -to 16-oz. pkg. cocktail wieners or small, cooked smoked sausage links

1. Remove ½ teaspoon zest and squeeze 1 tablespoon juice from lime. In a 1½-quart slow cooker combine lime zest and juice and next five ingredients (through hot pepper sauce). Stir in wieners.
2. Cover and cook on low 4 hours. Serve immediately or keep warm, covered, on warm or low up to 2 hours. Makes 14 servings.
Note Some 1½-quart slow cookers include variable heat settings; others have only one (low) setting. For cookers with no heat settings, check manufacturer's guidelines for timing.
PER SERVING 160 cal, 8 g fat (3 g sat. fat), 25 mg chol., 342 mg sodium, 20 g carb., 0 g fiber, 13 g sugars, 3 g pro.

TURKEY-SAGE SPANAKOPITA

SAUSAGE-PESTO
PULL-APART BREAD

SAUSAGE-PESTO PULL-APART BREAD

PREP 25 minutes
RISE 1 hour 15 minutes
BAKE 45 minutes at 350°F
COOL 10 minutes

- ¾ cup milk
- 1 pkg. active dry yeast
- 1 egg, lightly beaten
- ¼ cup butter, melted
- 1 Tbsp. granulated sugar
- ½ tsp. salt
- 3 cups all-purpose flour
- ⅓ cup plus 1 Tbsp. purchased basil pesto
- 8 oz. Italian sausage, cooked, drained, and crumbled
- ½ cup chopped roasted red sweet peppers
- 1½ cups shredded mozzarella cheese (6 oz.)
- 1 Tbsp. olive oil

1. In a small saucepan heat the milk just until warm (105°F to 115°F). In a large bowl combine warm milk and yeast; stir until yeast is dissolved. Let stand 5 minutes.
2. Add egg, the ¼ cup melted butter, sugar, and salt to the yeast mixture. Beat with a mixer on medium until combined. Add half the flour; beat on low 30 seconds, scraping bowl as needed. Beat 1 minute on medium. Stir in remaining flour. Shape dough into a ball (dough will not be smooth). Place dough in a greased bowl; turn once to grease surface. Cover and let rise in a warm place until nearly double in size (45 to 60 minutes).
3. Grease a 9×5-inch loaf pan. Turn dough out onto a lightly floured surface. Roll into a 20×12-inch rectangle. Stir together ⅓ cup pesto and the sausage; spread over dough. Sprinkle with red peppers and cheese. Cut rectangle in half lengthwise to make two 20×6-inch strips. Cut each strip crosswise into five 6×4-inch strips. Carefully make two stacks of five strips each. Cut each stack into 4×2-inch pieces. Loosely stagger pieces in pan, cut sides up. Cover and let rise in a warm place until nearly double in size (30 minutes).
4. Preheat oven to 350°F. Bake 45 minutes or until golden brown and an instant-read thermometer inserted near center registers 200°F. Cool in pan 10 minutes. Transfer to a serving plate. In a small bowl combine remaining pesto and oil. Drizzle over loaf. Makes 10 servings.

PER SERVING 368 cal., 20 g fat (8 g sat. fat), 59 mg chol., 550 mg sodium, 33 g carb., 1 g fiber, 3 g sugars, 12 g pro.

KALE-WHITE CHEDDAR GALETTE
(PICTURED ON PAGE 28)

PREP 25 minutes
BAKE 35 minutes at 375°F

- 1 recipe Pastry for Single-Crust Pie
- 3 Tbsp. olive oil
- 1 shallot, thinly sliced
- 1 clove garlic, minced
- 10 cups chopped, stemmed kale
- 2 Tbsp. chopped fresh sage
- ¼ tsp. salt
- ½ cup shredded white cheddar cheese (2 oz.)
  Milk (optional)
- ½ lemon

1. Preheat oven to 375°F. Prepare pastry. On a large piece of lightly floured parchment paper, roll pastry to a 13-inch circle. Slide parchment and pastry onto a baking sheet. Set aside.
2. For filling, in an extra-large skillet heat 2 tablespoons oil over medium heat. Add shallot and garlic. Cook and stir 2 minutes or until shallot is softened. Add kale; toss 4 to 5 minutes or just until wilted. Stir in sage and ¼ teaspoon salt.
3. Spread kale mixture on center of pastry, leaving 1½-inch border. Using parchment, lift and fold pastry edge over filling, pleating edges. Sprinkle filling with cheese. If desired, brush pastry with milk.
4. Bake 35 to 40 minutes or until crust is golden. Cool slightly before serving. Squeeze lemon over filling, drizzle with remaining oil, and sprinkle with additional chopped sage. Makes 6 servings.
Pastry for Single-Crust Pie In a medium bowl stir together 1½ cups all-purpose flour and ¼ teaspoon salt. Using a pastry blender, cut in ¼ cup shortening and ¼ cup butter, cut up, until pea size. Sprinkle 1 tablespoon ice water over part of the flour mixture; toss gently with a fork. Push moistened pastry to side of bowl. Repeat moistening, gradually adding ice water (¼ to ⅓ cup total) until pastry begins to come together. Gather pastry into a ball; knead gently just until it holds together.
PER SERVING 413 cal., 28 g fat (10 g sat. fat), 30 mg chol., 457 mg sodium, 35 g carb., 5 g fiber, 3 g sugars, 11 g pro.

PIMIENTO CHEESE

PREP 10 minutes
CHILL 4 hours

- 3 cups shredded cheddar cheese (12 oz.)
- ⅔ cup mayonnaise
- 1 4-oz. jar sliced pimiento, drained and chopped
- 1 tsp. Worcestershire sauce
- 1 tsp. yellow mustard
- ¼ tsp. garlic powder
  Assorted crackers

1. In a large bowl stir together cheese, mayonnaise, pimiento, Worcestershire, mustard, and garlic powder. Transfer to a serving bowl. Cover with plastic wrap and chill 4 to 24 hours. Serve as a spread with crackers. Makes 18 servings.
PER SERVING 137 cal., 13 g fat (5 g sat. fat), 23 mg chol., 169 mg sodium, 1 g carb., 0 g fiber, 0 g sugars, 5 g pro.
Jalapeño Cheese Prepare as directed, except omit pimiento and mustard. Substitute 6 ounces Colby and Monterey Jack cheese and 6 ounces Monterey Jack cheese with jalapeño peppers for the cheddar cheese. Stir one 4-ounce can diced jalapeño peppers, drained, into the cheese mixture.

Beef and Pickle Cheese Prepare as directed, except omit pimiento, Worcestershire, and mustard. Substitute Monterey Jack cheese for cheddar cheese. Add one 3-ounce package cream cheese, softened; ½ cup chopped dill pickle; and ½ cup chopped dried beef or boiled ham (about 2½ ounces) to cheese mixture. If desired, serve with melba toasts or rye crackers.

LOADED
POTATO DIP

TANGY SOUR CREAM
AND ONION DIP

LOADED POTATO DIP

PREP 30 minutes
SLOW COOK 2 hours (low)

1½ lb. Yukon gold or other yellow-flesh potatoes, peeled and quartered
4 slices hickory- or applewood-smoked bacon
1 8-oz. pkg. cream cheese, cubed and softened
¾ cup chicken broth
½ cup sour cream
¼ cup chopped green onions
¼ tsp. garlic salt
1 cup shredded sharp cheddar cheese (4 oz.)
Potato chips, sweet potato chips, and/or crackers

1. In a large covered saucepan cook potatoes in enough boiling, lightly salted water to cover 15 to 20 minutes or until tender; drain.
2. Meanwhile, in a large skillet cook bacon over medium heat until crisp. Drain on paper towels. Crumble bacon; reserve 1 tablespoon for topping.

3. In a medium bowl combine the next five ingredients (through garlic salt). Stir in the remaining bacon and ¾ cup of the cheddar cheese. Mash potatoes; stir into cheese mixture. Transfer to a 1½- or 2-quart slow cooker.
4. Cover and cook on low 2 hours or until heated through (thermometer registers 160°F). Sprinkle with remaining ¼ cup cheddar cheese and reserved bacon. Serve immediately or keep warm, covered, on warm or low up to 2 hours. Serve with chips and/or crackers. Makes 38 servings.
PER SERVING *56 cal., 4 g fat (2 g sat. fat), 12 mg chol., 103 mg sodium, 3 g carb., 0 g fiber, 0 g sugars, 2 g pro.*

Bacon, Blue Cheese, and Potato Dip
Prepare as directed, except substitute 1 cup crumbled blue cheese (4 oz.) for the cheddar cheese. Serve with barbecue-flavor potato chips and/or celery sticks.

TANGY SOUR CREAM AND ONION DIP

PREP 30 minutes
CHILL 2 hours

2 Tbsp. olive oil
1 cup chopped onions
Pinch salt
Pinch sugar
1 clove garlic, minced
½ cup sour cream
½ cup mayonnaise
½ cup plain Greek yogurt
Black pepper
Cut-up vegetables and/or crackers

1. In a medium skillet heat oil over medium-low heat. Add onions and a pinch each salt and sugar. Cook 15 minutes or until lightly browned. Add garlic; cook 3 to 5 minutes or until onions are golden. Transfer to a bowl; cool 5 minutes.
2. Stir in sour cream, mayonnaise, and yogurt. Season to taste with salt and pepper. Chill 2 hours or up to 8 hours. Serve with vegetables and/or crackers. Makes 12 servings.
PER SERVING *113 cal., 11 g fat (3 g sat. fat), 10 mg chol., 113 mg sodium, 2 g carb., 0 g fiber, 1 g sugars, 1 g pro.*

GARLIC AND MUSTARD PRETZEL TWISTS

GARLIC AND MUSTARD PRETZEL TWISTS

PREP 10 minutes
BAKE 25 minutes at 300°F

¼ cup butter
3 Tbsp. Dijon honey mustard
1 Tbsp. bottled minced garlic

1 Tbsp. honey
1 tsp. dry mustard
¼ tsp. cayenne pepper
8 cups small pretzel twists

1. Preheat oven to 300°F. In a saucepan combine all ingredients except pretzels; cook and stir until butter is melted.
2. Line a shallow roasting pan with heavy-duty foil; place pretzels in pan.

Pour butter mixture over pretzels; toss gently to coat.
3. Bake 25 minutes, stirring twice. Spread on foil to cool. Makes 16 servings.
PER SERVING *111 cal., 3 g fat (2 g sat. fat), 8 mg chol., 363 mg sodium, 19 g carb., 1 g fiber, 2 g sugars, 2 g pro.*

CHILE PEPPER–CHEESE BISCOTTI

CHILE PEPPER-CHEESE BISCOTTI

PREP 30 minutes
COOL 1 hour
BAKE 30 minutes at 350°F/27 minutes at 325°F

1   cup shredded white cheddar cheese (4 oz.)
¼   cup butter, softened
1   4-oz. can diced green chile peppers, undrained
2½ tsp. baking powder
¼   tsp. salt
¼   tsp. black pepper
2   eggs
½   cup yellow cornmeal
2   cups all-purpose flour
    Sliced Monterey Jack cheese with jalapeño peppers (optional)
    Bottled sliced pickled jalapeño chile peppers (optional)

1. Preheat oven to 350°F. Lightly grease a cookie sheet; set aside. In a large bowl combine cheddar cheese and butter. Beat with a mixer on medium to high 30 seconds. Add diced chile peppers, baking powder, salt, and black pepper; beat until combined. Beat in eggs. Beat in cornmeal. Beat in as much of the flour as you can with the mixer. Stir or knead in any remaining flour.
2. Divide dough in half. Shape each portion into a 9-inch roll. Place rolls about 5 inches apart on prepared cookie sheet; slightly flatten each roll to about 3 inches wide.
3. Bake 30 to 35 minutes or until lightly browned. Cool on cookie sheet 1 hour.
4. Preheat oven to 325°F. Using a serrated knife, cut each roll diagonally into ¼-inch slices. Place slices on an ungreased cookie sheet. Bake 15 minutes. Turn slices over and bake 12 to 15 minutes more or until biscotti are dry and crisp (do not overbake). Transfer to a wire rack; cool.
5. If desired, serve biscotti with Monterey Jack cheese and pickled jalapeño peppers. Makes 56 servings.
PER SERVING *40 cal., 2 g fat (1 g sat. fat), 12 mg chol., 50 mg sodium, 4 g carb., 0 g fiber, 0 g sugars, 1 g pro.*
To Store Layer biscotti between sheets of waxed paper in an airtight container; cover. Store in the refrigerator up to 3 days or freeze up to 2 weeks.

CRUNCHY NUT
SNACK MIX

BARBECUE SPICED ROASTED CHICKPEAS

PREP 5 minutes
ROAST 30 minutes at 450°F

- 2 15-oz. cans no-salt-added garbanzo beans (chickpeas), rinsed and drained
- ¼ cup olive oil
- 1 tsp. barbecue spice
- 1 tsp. paprika
- 1 tsp. chili powder
- ¼ tsp. garlic salt
- ¼ tsp. celery salt
- ¼ tsp. onion powder

1. Preheat oven to 450°F. In a medium bowl combine all ingredients. Spread in an even layer in a 15×10-inch baking pan.
2. Roast 30 minutes or until browned and crisp, stirring once. Cool completely. Makes 12 servings.
PER SERVING *101 cal., 5 g fat (1 g sat. fat), 0 mg chol., 122 mg sodium, 10 g carb., 3 g fiber, 0 g sugars, 4 g pro.*

CRUNCHY NUT SNACK MIX

PREP 10 minutes
SLOW COOK 1 hour 30 minutes (high) plus 20 minutes (low)

- Nonstick cooking spray
- 2 cups round toasted oat cereal
- 2 cups bite-size wheat square cereal
- 2 cups bite-size corn square cereal
- ¾ cup slivered almonds
- ⅓ cup packed brown sugar
- ⅓ cup butter, melted
- ¼ cup maple syrup
- 1 tsp. vanilla
- ½ tsp. ground cinnamon
- 1 cup dried apricots, coarsely chopped; dried cranberries or cherries; and/or golden raisins

1. Lightly coat a 6-quart slow cooker with cooking spray. Combine cereals and almonds in the cooker. In a small bowl combine next five ingredients (through cinnamon). Pour over cereal mixture; toss to coat.
2. Cover and cook on high 1½ hours, stirring up from bottom every 30 minutes. Turn to low. Cook, uncovered, 20 minutes more or until dry and crisp, stirring up from bottom every 10 minutes. Spread mix on a large piece of foil; sprinkle with dried fruit. Cool. Makes 12 servings.
PER SERVING *203 cal., 9 g fat (4 g sat. fat), 14 mg chol., 143 mg sodium, 30 g carb., 3 g fiber, 17 g sugars, 3 g pro.*

HOT CRANBERRY PUNCH

START TO FINISH 25 minutes

6   cups water
4   cups fresh or frozen cranberries
⅓   to ½ cup sugar
2   2-inch sticks cinnamon
10   whole cloves
1   lemon
2   black tea bags
½   tsp. orange zest
½   cup rum (optional)
     Fresh bay leaves (optional)

1. In a large saucepan bring the water to boiling. Add cranberries. Boil gently 3 to 4 minutes or until skins burst. Pour mixture through a fine-mesh sieve, pressing lightly on cranberries; discard solids.

2. Return strained liquid to saucepan. Stir in sugar, cinnamon sticks, and cloves. Bring to boiling, stirring to dissolve sugar. Reduce heat. Simmer, uncovered, 5 minutes. Remove from heat.

3. Remove ½ teaspoon zest and squeeze 1 tablespoon juice from lemon. Add tea bags, lemon zest and juice, and orange zest. Let stand 3 minutes; discard tea bags. If desired, stir in rum. Transfer to a punch bowl. If desired, top with additional cranberries and bay leaves. Makes 5 servings.

PER SERVING *134 cal., 5 g fat (3 g sat. fat), 12 mg chol., 47 mg sodium, 24 g carb., 3 g fiber, 17 g sugars, 0 g pro.*

WHITE CHRISTMAS PUNCH

PREP 20 minutes
FREEZE 4 hours

     Cranberries, orange slices, and bay leaves
1   qt. cinnamon or vanilla ice cream
⅔   cup bourbon
⅓   cup light rum
4   cups milk
     Ground cinnamon (optional)
     Orange slices (optional)

1. For ice ring wreath, arrange fruit in a 6-cup ring mold. Add bay leaves. Add just enough water to cover the fruit. Freeze just until firm. Add water to fill the ice ring. Cover and freeze until firm.

2. Meanwhile, in a large bowl stir the ice cream to soften. Stir in the bourbon and rum. Cover and freeze until needed (mixture will not freeze firm). To serve, place ice cream mixture in a punch bowl; blend in milk. Unmold ice ring and add to punch. if desired, sprinkle punch and servings with cinnamon. Garnish glass rims with an orange slice, if desired. Makes 12 servings.

PER SERVING *183 cal., 7 g fat (4 g sat. fat), 28 mg chol., 77 mg sodium, 15 g carb., 0 g fiber, 14 g sugars, 4 g pro.*

HOT CRANBERRY PUNCH

WHITE CHRISTMAS
PUNCH

DOUBLE-HOT DRINKING
CHOCOLATE, PAGE 59

Luscious Brunch

For Christmas morning or any day, these sweet and savory dishes are a lovely way to start the day. Choose from cheese-and meat-filled casseroles and bread puddings, light-as-a-feather donuts, sweet rolls, hot chocolate, creamy Mexican coffee, and sparkling mimosa.

PEANUT BUTTER
AND JELLY
BREAKFAST ROLLS,
PAGE 48

COCONUT-PECAN COFFEE CAKE

PREP 30 minutes
BAKE 55 minutes at 325°F
COOL 10 minutes

½   cup butter, softened
1   cup granulated sugar
2   tsp. baking powder
½   tsp. baking soda
¼   tsp. salt
2   eggs
1   tsp. vanilla
2¼ cups all-purpose flour
1   8-oz. carton sour cream
1   recipe Coconut-Pecan Topping
    Powdered sugar and unsweetened
    cocoa powder (optional)

1. Preheat oven to 325°F. Grease and
flour a 10-inch fluted tube pan; set aside.
In a large mixing bowl beat butter with
a mixer on medium 30 seconds. Add the
sugar, baking powder, baking soda, and
salt. Beat until well combined, scraping
sides of bowl occasionally. Add eggs,
one at a time, beating well after each
addition. Beat in vanilla. Alternately add
flour and sour cream, beating on low
after each addition just until combined.
2. Sprinkle half the Coconut-Pecan
Topping in the prepared pan. Spoon half
the batter in mounds over the coconut
mixture; carefully spread evenly. Sprinkle
with remaining topping. Spoon on
remaining batter, spreading evenly.
3. Bake 55 to 65 minutes or until a wooden
toothpick inserted near center comes
out clean. Cool in pan on a wire rack
10 minutes. Remove cake from pan; cool
completely on wire rack. If desired, dust
with a mixture of powdered sugar and
cocoa powder. Makes 12 servings.
Coconut-Pecan Topping In a large bowl
combine 1 cup all-purpose flour, 1 cup
packed brown sugar, and 1 teaspoon
ground cinnamon. Using a pastry
blender, cut in ½ cup cold butter, cut up,
until mixture resembles coarse crumbs.
Stir in ¾ cup semisweet chocolate
pieces, ½ cup flaked coconut, and ½ cup
chopped pecans.
PER SERVING *550 cal., 28 g fat (16 g sat. fat),
86 mg chol., 297 mg sodium, 71 g carb.,
2 g fiber, 43 g sugars, 6 g pro.*

**TOFFEE PUMPKIN
SNACK CAKE**

TOFFEE PUMPKIN SNACK CAKE

PREP 20 minutes
BAKE 30 minutes at 350°F

1½ cups sugar
¾   cup all-purpose flour
⅔   cup buckwheat flour or whole
    wheat flour
½   cup spelt flour or whole wheat flour
¼   cup flax seeds, hemp seeds,
    and/or chia seeds
2   tsp. baking powder
2   tsp. pumpkin pie spice
1   tsp. baking soda
½   tsp. salt
4   eggs, lightly beaten
1   15-oz. can pumpkin
1   cup vegetable oil
1   cup toffee pieces
1   recipe Cream Cheese Icing Drizzle

1. Preheat oven to 350°F. In a large bowl
stir together the first nine ingredients
(through salt). Add eggs, pumpkin, and
oil; stir until combined. Stir in ½ cup of
the toffee pieces. Spread batter in an
ungreased 13×9-inch baking pan. Sprinkle
with remaining toffee pieces.
2. Bake 30 minutes or until a toothpick
comes out clean. Cool in pan on a wire
rack. Spoon Cream Cheese Icing Drizzle
over cake. Makes 24 servings.
Cream Cheese Icing Drizzle In a medium
bowl beat 2 ounces softened cream
cheese and 1 tablespoon softened butter
with a mixer on medium until smooth. Beat
in ¾ cup powdered sugar and enough
milk (2 to 3 tablespoons) to make drizzling
consistency. Makes about ¾ cup.
PER SERVING *265 cal., 15 g fat (4 g sat. fat),
41 mg chol., 206 mg sodium, 31 g carb.,
2 g fiber, 22 g sugars, 3 g pro.*

APPLE SCONES WITH SPICED MAPLE BUTTER

PREP 30 minutes
BAKE 15 minutes at 400°F
COOL 5 minutes

2¾ cups all-purpose flour
½ cup granulated sugar
1 Tbsp. baking powder
1 tsp. apple pie spice
½ tsp. salt
½ cup butter, chilled and cut into small pieces
1 cup finely chopped tart apple, such as Braeburn, Jonagold, or Granny Smith
2 eggs, lightly beaten
¾ cup heavy cream
1 egg yolk, lightly beaten
1 Tbsp. heavy cream
1 small Braeburn or Jonathan apple, cored and thinly sliced
Coarse sugar or granulated sugar
1 recipe Spiced Maple Butter or honey

1. Preheat oven to 400°F. Line an extra-large baking sheet with parchment paper or foil. In a large bowl combine the first five ingredients (through salt). Using a pastry blender cut in cold butter until mixture resembles coarse crumbs. Stir in the 1 cup finely chopped apple. Make a well in center of flour mixture.

2. In a small bowl combine the 2 eggs and ¾ cup heavy cream. Using a fork stir egg mixture into flour mixture just until moistened. Turn dough out onto a floured surface. Knead dough by folding and gently pressing 10 to 12 strokes or until nearly smooth. Divide in half. Pat or lightly roll each half into a 6-inch circle. Cut each circle into six wedges. Place wedges on prepared baking sheet.

3. In a small bowl combine the egg yolk and 1 tablespoon heavy cream. Brush some yolk mixture on wedges. Arrange apple slices on wedges, pressing lightly to adhere. Brush with remaining yolk mixture; sprinkle with coarse sugar.

4. Bake 15 to 18 minutes or until lightly browned. Cool on baking sheet 5 minutes. Serve warm with Spiced Maple Butter. Makes 12 servings.

Spiced Maple Butter In a small bowl stir together ½ cup butter, softened; 3 tablespoons pure maple syrup or 2 tablespoons mild honey; and ¼ teaspoon apple pie spice or ground cinnamon until smooth. Cover and chill up to 1 week. Serve at room temperature. Makes ⅔ cup.

PER SERVING *372 cal., 23 g fat (14 g sat. fat), 105 mg chol., 359 mg sodium, 38 g carb., 1 g fiber, 15 g sugars, 5 g pro.*

CHOCOLATE CAKE DONUTS

PREP 20 minutes
BAKE 10 minutes at 325°F
COOL 3 minutes

Nonstick cooking spray
1 cup white whole wheat flour
¼ cup unsweetened cocoa powder
½ tsp. baking soda
¼ tsp. salt
½ cup packed brown sugar
½ cup vanilla low-fat yogurt
¼ cup refrigerated or frozen egg product, thawed
2 Tbsp. canola oil
1 tsp. vanilla
½ cup powdered sugar
1 Tbsp. unsweetened cocoa powder
1 Tbsp. milk
2 tsp. sprinkles or nonpareils

1. Preheat oven to 325°F. Coat a mini donut pan with cooking spray;* set aside.
2. In a large bowl stir together flour, ¼ cup cocoa powder, baking soda, and salt. In a small bowl combine brown sugar, yogurt,

APPLE SCONES WITH SPICED MAPLE BUTTER

CHOCOLATE CAKE DONUTS

egg, oil, and vanilla. Add yogurt mixture to flour mixture, stirring until smooth.

3. Spoon batter into a large resealable plastic bag. Cut off one corner of the bag; squeeze batter into the prepared indentations in donut pan, filling each about two-thirds full. Smooth tops. Bake 10 minutes or until donuts are nearly firm when lightly pressed. Cool in pan on a wire rack 3 minutes. Remove donuts from pan. Cool completely on wire rack.

4. For icing, in a small bowl stir together powdered sugar, 1 tablespoon cocoa powder, and milk until smooth. Dip cooled doughnuts into icing, allowing excess to drip back into bowl. Return donuts to wire rack. Top with sprinkles. Makes 10 servings.
PER SERVING *146 cal., 3 g fat (0 g sat. fat), 0 mg chol., 143 mg sodium, 28 g carb., 2 g fiber, 17 g sugars, 3 g pro.*

*Tip If necessary, bake donuts in two batches, washing pan and recoating with cooking spray before adding remaining batter.
Note If you prefer, instead of icing, gently toss warm donuts in a mixture of powdered sugar and unsweetened cocoa powder.

CINNAMON-SUGAR BOURBON-PUMPKIN MUFFINS

PREP 25 minutes
BAKE 25 minutes at 350°F
COOL 10 minutes

3⅓ cups sugar
¾ cup finely chopped pecans
2 tsp. ground cinnamon
2¾ cups all-purpose flour
2 tsp. baking soda
1 tsp. salt
1 15-oz. can pumpkin
¾ cup vegetable oil
3 eggs
¼ cup bourbon or water
1 recipe Bourbon Icing (optional)

1. Preheat oven to 350°F. Line twenty-four 2½-inch muffin cups with paper bake cups. In a small bowl combine ⅔ cup of the sugar, the pecans, and 1 teaspoon of the cinnamon; set aside. In an extra-large bowl stir together flour, baking soda, salt, and the remaining 1 teaspoon cinnamon. Make a well in center of flour mixture.
2. In a large bowl whisk together the remaining 2⅔ cups sugar, the pumpkin, oil, eggs, and bourbon. Add egg mixture all at once to flour mixture. Stir just until moistened. Spoon batter into prepared muffin cups, filling each about three-fourths full. Sprinkle with nut mixture.
3. Bake 25 to 28 minutes or until a toothpick comes out clean. Cool in muffin cups 10 minutes. Remove; cool on wire racks. If desired, drizzle with Bourbon Icing before serving. Makes 24 servings.
PER SERVING *265 cal., 10 g fat (1 g sat. fat), 23 mg chol., 212 mg sodium, 41 g carb., 1 g fiber, 29 g sugars, 3 g pro.*
Bourbon Icing In a small bowl stir together 1 cup powdered sugar, 1 tablespoon bourbon, and enough milk (2 to 3 teaspoons) to make drizzling consistency.

PEANUT BUTTER AND JELLY BREAKFAST ROLLS

PREP 45 minutes
RISE 1 hour 30 minutes
BAKE 30 minutes at 375°F
COOL 5 minutes

4¼ to 4¾ cups all-purpose flour
1 pkg. active dry yeast
1¼ cups milk
¼ cup butter, cut up
⅓ cup granulated sugar
1 tsp. salt
2 eggs
¾ cup creamy peanut butter
¼ cup strawberry, raspberry, or grape jam or jelly, melted
1 recipe Peanut Butter Icing

1. In a large bowl combine 1½ cups of the flour and the yeast. In a saucepan heat and stir milk, butter, sugar, and salt just until warm (120°F to 130°F) and butter is almost melted; add to flour mixture along with the eggs and ¼ cup of the peanut butter. Beat with a mixer on low 30 seconds, scraping bowl as needed. Beat on high 3 minutes. Stir in as much of the remaining flour as you can.
2. Turn dough out onto a lightly floured surface. Knead in enough of the remaining flour to make a moderately soft dough that is smooth and elastic (3 to 5 minutes total). Shape dough into a ball. Place dough in a lightly greased bowl, turning once to grease surface of the dough. Cover; let rise in a warm place until double in size (about 1 hour).
3. Punch down dough. Turn out onto a lightly floured surface. Cover; let rest 10 minutes. Meanwhile, lightly grease a 13×9-inch baking pan. For filling, in a small bowl stir together the remaining ½ cup peanut butter and the ¼ cup jam or jelly.
4. Roll dough into an 18×12-inch rectangle. Spread filling on dough, leaving 1 inch unfilled along one long side. Roll up rectangle, starting from the filled long side; pinch dough to seal seam. Slice into 12 pieces. Arrange rolls, cut sides up, in the prepared pan. Cover; let rise in a warm place until nearly double in size (about 30 minutes).
5. Preheat oven to 375°F. Bake 30 minutes or until golden. Cool 5 minutes. Carefully invert rolls onto a wire rack; cool slightly. Invert again onto a serving platter. Spread with Peanut Butter Icing. If desired, drizzle additional melted jam or jelly over the frosting. Makes 12 servings.
Peanut Butter Icing In a medium bowl combine 1½ cups powdered sugar and 3 tablespoons creamy peanut butter. Stir in 4 tablespoons milk. If needed, stir in an additional 1 tablespoon milk, 1 teaspoon at a time, until spreading consistency.
PER SERVING *442 cal., 16 g fat (5 g sat. fat), 44 mg chol., 339 mg sodium, 65 g carb., 2 g fiber, 28 g sugars, 11 g pro.*

CARAMEL-BANANA-PECAN BREAD CASSEROLE

PREP 25 minutes
SLOW COOK 4 hours (low)
STAND 30 minutes

1 12-oz. loaf French bread, cut into 1-inch cubes (about 9 cups)
3 eggs, lightly beaten
2 cups half-and-half or whole milk
¼ cup granulated sugar
1 Tbsp. vanilla
½ tsp. ground cinnamon
⅛ tsp. ground nutmeg
¼ cup packed brown sugar
2 Tbsp. butter
1 cup pecans, coarsely chopped and toasted*
1 recipe Caramel-Banana Sauce

1. Preheat oven to 300°F. Arrange bread cubes in a single layer in a baking pan. Bake 10 to 15 minutes or until golden, stirring once or twice. Cool.
2. Line a 3½- or 4-quart slow cooker with a disposable slow cooker liner. Place bread cubes in prepared cooker. In a medium bowl combine the next six ingredients (through nutmeg); pour over

PEANUT BUTTER AND JELLY BREAKFAST ROLLS

CARAMEL-BANANA-PECAN BREAD CASSEROLE

bread cubes. Use a large spoon to lightly press down bread to moisten.

3. Place brown sugar in a medium bowl. Use a pastry blender to cut butter into brown sugar until pea size. Stir in pecans. Sprinkle over bread mixture.

4. Cover and cook on low 4 to 5 hours or until a knife comes out clean. Turn off cooker. If possible, remove crockery liner from cooker. Let stand, covered, 30 minutes. Serve with Caramel-Banana Sauce. Makes 8 servings.

Caramel-Banana Sauce In a medium-size heavy saucepan combine ¾ cup packed brown sugar, ½ cup heavy cream, ½ cup cut-up butter, and 2 tablespoons light-color corn syrup. Bring to boiling over medium-high heat, whisking occasionally; reduce heat to medium. Boil gently, uncovered, 3 minutes. Remove from heat. Stir in 1 teaspoon vanilla. Pour sauce into a small bowl; cool to room temperature. If desired, cover and chill overnight. To serve, let chilled sauce stand at room

temperature 1 hour. Stir in 1 banana, thinly sliced.

*Tip To toast whole nuts or large pieces, preheat oven to 350°F. Spread nuts in an even layer in a large baking pan. Bake 5 to 10 minutes or until lightly browned, shaking the pan once or twice.

PER SERVING *658 cal., 39 g fat (19 g sat. fat), 160 mg chol., 445 mg sodium, 68 g carb., 3 g fiber, 38 g sugars, 11 g pro.*

CHEDDAR AND BACON BREAD PUDDING

PREP 20 minutes
BAKE 45 minutes at 350°F
COOL 20 minutes

4   cups dried garlic focaccia or Italian bread*
½   cup crisp-cooked and crumbled bacon
¾   cup shredded yellow or white cheddar cheese
2   eggs, lightly beaten
1¾   cups milk
¼   cup butter, melted
1   tsp. dried Italian seasoning, crushed
¼   tsp. salt

1. Preheat oven to 350°F. Grease a 2-quart square baking dish. Place dried bread, bacon, and half the cheese in the dish. In a medium bowl whisk together eggs, milk, butter, Italian seasoning, and salt. Pour over bread mixture in dish. Use a spatula to press bread into the milk mixture.
2. Bake, uncovered, 45 to 50 minutes or until puffed and a knife inserted near center comes out clean. Top with remaining cheese. Cool about 20 minutes. Serve warm. Makes 8 servings.
PER SERVING *237 cal., 16 g fat (3 g sat. fat), 84 mg chol., 502 mg sodium, 12 g carb., 0 g fiber, 3 g sugars, 11 g pro.*
*Tip To dry bread cubes, preheat oven to 300°F. Arrange cubes in a single layer on a baking sheet. Bake 10 to 15 minutes or until golden, stirring once or twice.

EGGNOG FRENCH TOAST BREAD PUDDING

EGGNOG FRENCH TOAST BREAD PUDDING

PREP 20 minutes
CHILL 4 hours
SLOW COOK 3 hours (low)
STAND 30 minutes

9   cups 1-inch challah or Hawaiian sweet bread cubes
     Nonstick cooking spray
3   eggs, lightly beaten
3   cups eggnog
¼   cup sugar
1   tsp. ground nutmeg
1   tsp. vanilla
¼   tsp. salt
     Maple syrup

1. Preheat oven to 300°F. Spread bread cubes in two 15×10-inch baking pans. Bake 10 to 15 minutes or until dry, stirring twice. Cool. (Or let bread cubes stand, loosely covered, at room temperature 8 to 10 hours.)
2. Line a 3½- or 4-quart oval slow cooker with a disposable slow cooker liner; coat liner with cooking spray. Place bread cubes in prepared cooker.
3. In a large bowl whisk together the next six ingredients (through salt); pour over bread cubes. Use a large spoon to lightly press down bread to moisten. Cover; chill 4 to 24 hours.
4. Cover and cook on low 3 hours or until a knife comes out clean, giving crockery liner a half-turn halfway through cooking, if possible. Turn off cooker. If possible, remove crockery liner from cooker. Let stand, covered, 30 minutes. Serve with maple syrup. Makes 8 servings.
PER SERVING *296 cal., 7 g fat (3 g sat. fat), 141 mg chol., 336 mg sodium, 47 g carb., 2 g fiber, 29 g sugars, 11 g pro.*

CHEDDAR AND BACON
BREAD PUDDING

SPINACH-PANCETTA
QUICHE

SPINACH-PANCETTA QUICHE

PREP 1 hour
CHILL 30 minutes
ROAST 30 minutes at 400°F
BAKE 80 minutes at 325°F
COOL 40 minutes

1	recipe Deep-Dish Pastry Shell
8	oz. pancetta, chopped
2	large onions, thinly sliced
½	tsp. dried thyme, crushed
½	cup oil-packed dried tomatoes, drained and chopped
4	cups fresh baby spinach
2	cups shredded Havarti cheese (8 oz.)
6	eggs
2	cups plain fat-free Greek yogurt
1	cup milk
½	tsp. salt
¼	tsp. white pepper
⅛	tsp. ground nutmeg
	Fresh basil (optional)

1. Prepare Deep-Dish Pastry Shell. Preheat oven to 400°F. Line the inside of the shell with a double thickness of heavy-duty foil. Bake 20 minutes or until edge of pastry is lightly browned. Remove foil; bake 10 to 15 minutes more or until bottom is lightly browned. Cool completely on a wire rack.
2. In a large skillet cook pancetta over medium heat 10 to 12 minutes or until lightly browned, stirring occasionally. Using a slotted spoon, drain on paper towels, reserving 2 tablespoons drippings in skillet. Add onions and thyme; cook over medium heat 20 to 22 minutes or until golden, stirring occasionally. Stir in dried tomatoes; cook 1 minute. Add spinach; cook 1 to 2 minutes or until wilted. Cool 10 minutes. Stir in pancetta and cheese.
3. Meanwhile, preheat oven to 325°F. In a blender combine eggs, yogurt, milk, salt, pepper, and nutmeg. Cover and blend until frothy. Spoon onion mixture into pastry shell; add egg mixture. Place springform pan in a shallow baking pan.
4. Bake 80 to 90 minutes or just until top is lightly browned and filling is set in center (165°F). Cool in pan on a wire rack 40 minutes. Using a serrated knife, trim pastry flush with top of pan. Remove sides of pan. If desired, sprinkle quiche with basil. Makes 10 servings.
Deep-Dish Pastry Shell In a food processor combine 2 cups all-purpose flour and 1 teaspoon salt. Add

CARAMELIZED ONION AND POTATO BREAKFAST CASSEROLE

8 tablespoons cold unsalted butter, cut into small pieces; cover and pulse until mixture resembles coarse crumbs. Combine 1 lightly beaten egg and ¼ cup cold water; add to flour mixture. Cover and pulse just until pastry begins to stick together. Transfer to plastic wrap. Cover; shape into a disk. Chill at least 30 minutes. On a lightly floured surface, roll pastry into a 15-inch circle. Transfer to a 9-inch springform pan; gently press into pan. Trim overhanging pastry to 1 inch and press firmly against edge. Fill any cracks with trimmings. Freeze pastry shell 20 minutes.

PER SERVING *455 cal., 27 g fat (14 g sat. fat), 182 mg chol., 728 mg sodium, 28 g carb., 2 g fiber, 5 g sugars, 22 g pro.*

CARAMELIZED ONION AND POTATO BREAKFAST CASSEROLE

PREP 45 minutes
BAKE 45 minutes at 350°F
STAND 15 minutes

4	cups sliced golden potatoes, cut ⅛ to ¼ inch thick (about 1½ lb.)
1	Tbsp. olive oil
2	oz. pancetta, chopped
3	cups thinly sliced sweet onions, such as Vidalia or Maui Butter
6	eggs, lightly beaten
½	cup milk
1	cup shredded Gruyère cheese or Swiss cheese
1	tsp. salt
1	tsp. snipped fresh rosemary
½	tsp. black pepper

1. Preheat oven to 350°F. In a large saucepan cook potatoes, covered, in boiling lightly salted water 5 minutes or until slightly tender but still firm. Drain; set aside. In a large skillet heat olive oil over medium-high heat. Add pancetta; cook until lightly browned. Using a slotted spoon, transfer pancetta to paper towels to drain, reserving drippings in skillet. Add onions to skillet. Cook and stir over medium-low heat 20 minutes or until lightly browned and tender. Remove from heat. Carefully stir potatoes and pancetta into onions.
2. Lightly butter a 2-quart rectangular baking dish. Spread potato mixture into prepared dish. In a medium bowl whisk together eggs and milk. Add cheese, salt, rosemary, and pepper; stir until well mixed. Pour over potato mixture in baking dish.
3. Bake, uncovered, 45 to 50 minutes or until golden and a knife inserted in center comes out clean. Let stand 15 minutes before serving. Makes 8 servings.
PER SERVING *250 cal., 13 g fat (5 g sat. fat), 180 mg chol., 535 mg sodium, 22 g carb., 3 g fiber, 4 g sugars, 13 g pro.*
Make Ahead Prepare as directed through Step 2. Cover; chill up to 24 hours. Continue with Step 3.

GREENS, EGGS, AND HAM FRITTATA

PREP 20 minutes
BAKE 20 minutes at 350°F
COOL 10 minutes

10   large eggs
1½ cups shredded Monterey Jack cheese (6 oz.)
½   cup finely grated Romano or Parmesan cheese (2 oz.)
4   to 6 thin slices smoked ham, torn into pieces
¼   tsp. black pepper
2   Tbsp. butter
2   Tbsp. olive oil
1   large spring onion or 4 green onions, sliced into thin rounds
10 oz. mixed baby greens, such as chard, kale, and/or spinach

1. Preheat oven to 350°F. In a large bowl whisk together eggs, cheeses, ham, and pepper. In an oven-going 10-inch skillet heat 1 tablespoon of the butter and 1 tablespoon of the oil over medium heat until butter is melted. Add onion; cook and stir 2 minutes or until tender. Gradually add greens; cook and toss 2 minutes or until wilted. Transfer to a colander to drain, pressing out excess liquid. Stir greens into eggs.

2. In the same skillet heat remaining butter and oil over medium heat until butter is melted. Pour in egg mixture. Bake 20 minutes or until slightly puffed and set. Remove; let cool 10 minutes before serving. Makes 6 servings.

PER SERVING *342 cal., 27 g fat (12 g sat. fat), 356 mg chol., 498 mg sodium, 3 g carb., 1 g fiber, 1 g sugars, 21 g pro.*

BUTTERNUT SQUASH SHAKSHUKA

PREP 25 minutes
SLOW COOK 11 hours (low) or 5½ hours (high) plus 25 minutes (high)

¾   cup chopped red sweet pepper
1   small onion, halved and thinly sliced
1   medium jalapeño, seeded and finely chopped*
2   cloves garlic, minced
1   tsp. dried oregano, crushed
1   tsp. ground cumin
½   tsp. salt
½   tsp. black pepper
1   2-lb. butternut squash, peeled, seeded, and chopped (6 cups)
1   15-oz. can or ½ a 28-oz. can crushed tomatoes
1   8-oz. can tomato sauce
6   eggs
¾   cup crumbled feta cheese (3 oz.)
2   Tbsp. chopped fresh parsley
    Pita bread rounds, warmed

1. In a 3½- or 4-quart slow cooker combine the first eight ingredients (through black pepper). Stir in squash, crushed tomatoes, and tomato sauce.

2. Cover and cook on low 11 to 12 hours or high 5½ to 6 hours. If using low, turn to high. Break an egg into a custard cup. Make an indentation in squash mixture and slip egg into indentation. Repeat with remaining eggs. Cover and cook 25 to 35 minutes more or until eggs are desired doneness.

3. Top servings with cheese and parsley. Serve with pita bread. Makes 6 servings.

*Tip Chile peppers contain oils that can irritate skin and eyes. Wear plastic or rubber gloves when working with them.

PER SERVING *315 cal., 10 g fat (5 g sat. fat), 203 mg chol., 917 mg sodium, 45 g carb., 6 g fiber, 10 g sugars, 15 g pro.*

GREENS, EGGS, AND HAM FRITTATA

BUTTERNUT SQUASH SHAKSHUKA

MUSHROOM AND CHEESE SOURDOUGH TOASTS

START TO FINISH 30 minutes

- 2 Tbsp. extra-virgin olive oil plus 1 tsp.
- 1 Tbsp. butter
- 6 cups sliced assorted mushrooms
- 2 cloves garlic, minced
- 1 Tbsp. chopped fresh thyme
  Coarse salt and freshly ground black pepper
- 4 eggs

- 4 ½-inch thick slices rustic sourdough bread
- 2 cups sliced semisoft cheese, such as Taleggio or Fontina

1. Preheat broiler. In a large skillet heat the 2 tablespoons olive oil and the butter over medium-high heat. When butter is melted, add mushrooms and garlic. Cook 6 minutes or until mushrooms are tender and browned, stirring occasionally. Remove from heat. Season with thyme, salt, and pepper. Transfer to a bowl.
2. In the same skillet heat 1 teaspoon olive oil over medium heat. Break eggs into skillet. Reduce heat to low; cook eggs 3 to 4 minutes or until whites are completely set and yolks start to thicken.
3. Meanwhile, arrange bread slices on a baking sheet. Broil 4 inches from heat 1 minute on each side or until toasted. Place a slice of cheese on each bread slice; broil 1 minute more or until cheese is melted and starting to bubble. Remove from oven. Top cheese with mushroom mixture and eggs. Sprinkle with fresh herbs or microgreens. Makes 4 servings.
PER SERVING *482 cal., 33 g fat (15 g sat. fat), 259 mg chol., 759 mg sodium, 20 g carb., 2 g fiber, 5 g sugars, 28 g pro.*

MUSHROOM AND
CHEESE SOURDOUGH
TOASTS

UPSIDE-DOWN WAFFLE AND EGG CUPS

CREAMY AND LUSCIOUS FRUIT-FILLED CREPES

UPSIDE-DOWN WAFFLE AND EGG CUPS

PREP 15 minutes
BAKE 15 minutes at 375°F
COOL 5 minutes

- 12 frozen mini waffles, toasted according to package directions
- 2 cups shredded cheddar cheese (8 oz.)
- 1 9- to 10-oz. pkg. frozen cooked breakfast sausage links, thawed and chopped
- 6 eggs, lightly beaten
- 3 Tbsp. milk
- 2 Tbsp. grated Parmesan cheese
- ½ tsp. black pepper
- ¼ tsp. salt
   Maple syrup

1. Preheat oven to 375°F. Grease twelve 2½-inch muffin cups. Place mini waffles in prepared muffin cups. Sprinkle with 1 cup of the cheddar cheese. Top with sausage and remaining 1 cup cheddar cheese.
2. In a medium bowl combine the next five ingredients (through salt). Spoon over filling in muffin cups.
3. Bake 15 to 18 minutes or until set and golden. Cool on a wire rack 5 minutes. Remove from muffin cups. Drizzle with maple syrup. Makes 12 servings.
PER SERVING *221 cal., 15 g fat (6 g sat. fat), 131 mg chol., 443 mg sodium, 9 g carb., 0 g fiber, 5 g sugars, 12 g pro.*

Make Ahead Prepare as directed, except remove egg cups and cool completely. Place in a single layer in an airtight container. Refrigerate up to 5 days or freeze up to 3 months. To serve, microwave one egg cup at a time until heated through, allowing 15 to 20 seconds if chilled or 30 seconds if frozen.

CREAMY AND LUSCIOUS FRUIT-FILLED CREPES

START TO FINISH 40 minutes

- 1 egg, lightly beaten
- ¾ cup fat-free milk
- ½ cup all-purpose flour
- 1 Tbsp. olive oil
- ⅛ tsp. salt
   Nonstick cooking spray
- ⅓ cup plain Greek yogurt
- 1 tsp. honey
- ½ tsp. vanilla
   Milk
- 2 cups fresh fruit, such as peeled and sliced peaches, sliced strawberries, raspberries, blackberries, and/or blueberries
   Honey (optional)

1. For batter, in a medium bowl whisk together egg, the ¾ cup milk, the flour, oil, and salt until smooth. Lightly coat an 8-inch nonstick skillet with cooking spray; heat skillet over medium-high heat. Spoon about 2 tablespoons batter into skillet; lift and tilt skillet to spread batter evenly. Cook 1 to 2 minutes or until brown on one side. (Or cook on a crepemaker according to manufacturer's directions.) Invert over paper towels; remove crepe. Repeat with the remaining batter to make eight crepes total. If crepes brown too quickly, reduce heat to medium.
2. In a small bowl combine Greek yogurt, honey, and vanilla. Stir in milk, 1 teaspoon at a time, to reach desired consistency.
3. To assemble, place crepes, browned sides down, on a work surface. Spoon yogurt mixture and fruit onto half of each crepe. Fold unfilled half of crepe over filling. If desired, drizzle crepes with additional honey. Makes 4 servings.
PER SERVING *171 cal., 5 g fat (1 g sat. fat), 48 mg chol., 117 mg sodium, 23 g carb., 3 g fiber, 9 g sugars, 7 g pro.*

GRANOLA CUPS WITH YOGURT AND FRUIT

PREP 25 minutes
BAKE 15 minutes at 325°F

- 2 cups regular rolled oats
- ½ cup wheat germ
- ¼ cup dry-roasted sunflower kernels
- ¼ cup flaked coconut
- 2 Tbsp. flaxseeds
- ¼ cup butter
- ¼ cup packed dark brown sugar
- 2 Tbsp. honey or maple syrup
- ¼ tsp. ground cinnamon
- ½ tsp. vanilla

GRANOLA CUPS WITH YOGURT AND FRUIT

1   cup desired low-fat yogurt
1½ cups chopped fresh fruit and/or berries

1. In a large bowl combine the first five ingredients (through flaxseeds). In a small saucepan combine butter, brown sugar, honey, and cinnamon. Stir over medium heat until sugar is dissolved. Remove from heat. Stir in vanilla. Pour butter mixture over oat mixture; stir to coat. Cover and chill until cool.

2. Preheat oven to 325°F. Lightly grease twelve 2½-inch muffin cups. Using moist hands, press oat mixture onto bottoms and up sides of prepared muffin cups.
3. Bake 15 minutes or until edges are lightly browned. If centers puff during baking, repress with the back of a small spoon. Cool in muffin cups on a wire rack. Loosen and remove cups. Spoon yogurt into granola cups and top with fruit. Makes 12 servings.

PER SERVING *188 cal., 8 g fat (3 g sat. fat), 11 mg chol., 51 mg sodium, 26 g carb., 3 g fiber, 13 g sugars, 5 g pro.*
Make Ahead Prepare as directed, except do not fill granola cups. Layer granola cups between waxed paper in an airtight container. Store in refrigerator up to 3 days or freeze up to 3 months. To serve, thaw granola cups if frozen. Fill as directed.

MEXICAN COFFEE
EGGNOG

DOUBLE-HOT DRINKING CHOCOLATE

SPARKLING STRAWBERRY MIMOSA

MEXICAN COFFEE EGGNOG

PREP 25 minutes
CHILL 4 hours

- 8   egg yolks, lightly beaten
- 4   cups whole milk
- ½   cup sugar
- 1   stick cinnamon
- 10   whole roasted coffee or espresso beans
- 1   vanilla bean or 1 tsp. vanilla extract
- ⅓   to ½ cup light-color rum
- ¼   to ½ cup Kahlua or other coffee-flavor liqueur
       Ground nutmeg (optional)
       Whole roasted coffee or espresso beans (optional)

1. In a large heavy saucepan combine egg yolks, milk, sugar, stick cinnamon, the 10 coffee beans, and vanilla bean (if using). Cook and stir over medium heat 10 minutes or just until mixture coats a metal spoon. Remove from heat. Place the saucepan in a sink or bowl of ice water and stir milk mixture 2 minutes. Discard stick cinnamon and remove vanilla bean. (Do not remove coffee beans.) Using a sharp knife, halve vanilla bean lengthwise; use knife tip to scrape out seeds; discard vanilla bean pod. Transfer milk mixture to a pitcher.
2. Stir in rum, Kahlua, and vanilla extract (if using). Cover; chill 4 hours or up to 24 hours before serving. If desired, sprinkle with ground nutmeg and top

with additional coffee beans. Makes 10 servings.
PER SERVING *184 cal., 7 g fat (3 g sat. fat), 157 mg chol., 50 mg sodium, 18 g carb., 0 g fiber, 17 g sugars, 5 g pro.*

DOUBLE-HOT DRINKING CHOCOLATE

START TO FINISH 25 minutes

- 1½   cups whole milk
- 1   cup heavy cream
- 3   Tbsp. packed brown sugar
- 2   3×1-inch strips orange peel
- ⅛   tsp. cayenne pepper
- 10   oz. bittersweet chocolate, finely chopped
- ½   tsp. vanilla
       Unsweetened whipped cream

1. In a medium-size heavy saucepan, heat the milk, cream, brown sugar, orange peel, and cayenne over medium-low heat just until simmering. Remove from heat. Add chocolate and vanilla; let stand 5 minutes. Whisk until the mixture is smooth and chocolate is melted. Return to medium-low heat; heat and stir until desired temperature. Remove orange peel. Top servings with whipped cream and sprinkle with additional cayenne, if desired. Makes 8 servings.
PER SERVING *355 cal., 29 g fat (18 g sat. fat), 57 mg chol., 36 mg sodium, 28 g carb., 3 g fiber, 22 g sugars, 4 g pro.*

SPARKLING STRAWBERRY MIMOSA

START TO FINISH 15 minutes

- 4   cups strawberries, hulled and quartered
- 4   oranges, peeled and sectioned
- 1   750-ml. bottle champagne or sparkling apple juice, chilled
       Ice cubes
       Maple syrup (optional)

1. In a large pitcher combine strawberries and oranges. Muddle with a wooden spoon. Stir in champagne. Serve over ice. Drizzle with maple syrup, if desired. Makes 6 servings.
PER SERVING *186 cal., 0 fat, 0 mg chol., 2 mg sodium, 27 g carb., 4 g fiber, 19 g sugars, 2 g pro.*

CINNAMON ROLL
WREATH, PAGE 67

Fragrant Breads

Few aromas are as welcoming as bread baking in the oven. This collection features soft and buttery fantans, sweet pullaparts and rolls, crisp-crusted yeast breads, garlicky breadsticks, and tender scones. All are perfect for rousing sleepyheads or gift-giving.

MAPLE-MOCHA
PULLAPART BREAD
WITH ALMONDS

MAPLE-MOCHA PULLAPART BREAD WITH ALMONDS

PREP 45 minutes
RISE 1 hour 30 minutes
BAKE 40 minutes at 350°F
COOL 35 minutes

4	to 4½ cups all-purpose flour
¼	cup unsweetened cocoa powder
1	pkg. active dry yeast
1½	cups milk
¼	cup butter, cut up
¼	cup pure maple syrup
1	Tbsp. instant espresso coffee powder
1	tsp. salt
1	egg
1	cup heavy cream
1	Tbsp. butter
¾	cup pure maple syrup
1½	cups powdered sugar
1	to 2 Tbsp. milk
⅓	cup granulated sugar
½	tsp. ground cinnamon
⅔	cup sliced almonds, lightly toasted (tip, page 49)

1. In a large bowl combine 2 cups of the flour, the cocoa powder, and the yeast; set aside. In a medium saucepan heat and whisk together the next five ingredients (through salt) just until warm (120°F to 130°F) and butter is almost melted. Add milk mixture to flour mixture; add egg. Beat with a mixer on low 30 seconds, scraping bowl frequently. Beat on high 3 minutes. Stir in as much of the remaining flour as you can.
2. Turn dough out onto a lightly floured surface. Knead in enough of the remaining flour to make a soft dough that is smooth and elastic (3 to 5 minutes total). Shape dough into a ball. Place in a lightly greased bowl; turn to grease surface of dough. Cover; let rise in a warm place until double in size (about 1 hour).
3. While dough is rising, in a medium saucepan bring heavy cream to boiling; reduce heat. Boil gently, uncovered, 12 to 14 minutes or until reduced to ½ cup, stirring occasionally. Stir in 1 tablespoon butter. Cool 10 minutes. Gradually whisk in ¾ cup maple syrup. For icing, remove 3 tablespoons of the syrup mixture to a small bowl; stir in powdered sugar and enough milk to make a thick drizzling consistency; cover and set aside.

4. Punch dough down. Turn out onto a lightly floured surface. Divide into quarters. Cover and let rest 10 minutes. Meanwhile, in a small bowl combine granulated sugar and cinnamon. Generously grease a 10-inch fluted tube pan.

5. Roll each piece of dough into a rope about 20 inches long. Cut ropes into 1-inch pieces. Roll each piece in sugar-cinnamon mixture. Spoon half the remaining cooled syrup mixture into the prepared pan. Sprinkle with almonds. Arrange half the dough pieces on almonds. Sprinkle with half of the remaining sugar-cinnamon mixture. Drizzle remaining syrup mixture over dough in pan. Arrange remaining dough the pan. Sprinkle with remaining sugar-cinnamon mixture. Cover and let rise in a warm place until nearly double in size (30 to 45 minutes).

6. Preheat oven to 350°F. Bake 40 to 45 minutes (internal temperature should be 190°F to 200°F). Cool in pan 5 minutes. Loosen sides and center with a thin metal spatula or table knife. Invert onto a serving platter. Spoon any syrup and nuts that remain in pan over bread. Cool about 30 minutes. Drizzle with the maple icing before serving. Makes 16 servings.

PER SERVING *352 cal., 12 g fat (6 g sat. fat), 40 mg chol., 197 mg sodium, 56 g carb., 2 g fiber, 29 g sugars, 6 g pro.*

Make Ahead After assembling pull-apart bread in pan, cover with plastic wrap and chill 8 to 24 hours. Before baking, remove pan from refrigerator and let stand, covered, 1½ hours. Discard plastic wrap and bake at 350°F 45 minutes.

CINNAMON FANTANS

PREP 30 minutes
RISE 2 hours
BAKE 12 minutes at 350°F

2½ to 3 cups all-purpose flour
1   pkg. active dry yeast
¾   cup milk
¼   cup sugar
¼   cup butter
1   tsp. salt
1   egg
½   cup sugar
⅓   cup chopped walnuts
1½ tsp. ground cinnamon
2   Tbsp. butter, melted
    Powdered sugar (optional)
    Caramel ice cream topping
    (optional)

CINNAMON FANTANS

1. In a large bowl combine 1¼ cups of the flour and the yeast; set aside. In a small saucepan heat and stir milk, the ¼ cup sugar, ¼ cup butter, and salt just until warm (120°F to 130°F) and butter is almost melted. Add milk mixture to flour mixture; add egg. Beat with a mixer on low 30 seconds, scraping bowl constantly. Beat on high 3 minutes. Stir in as much of the remaining flour as you can.

2. Turn dough out onto a lightly floured surface. Knead in enough of the remaining flour to make a moderately soft dough that is smooth and elastic (3 to 5 minutes total). Shape dough into a ball. Place in a lightly greased bowl; turn once to grease surface of dough. Cover and let rise in a warm place until double in size (about 1½ hours).

3. Punch dough down. Turn out onto a lightly floured surface. Cover; let rest 10 minutes. Meanwhile, lightly grease a baking sheet. For filling, combine ½ cup sugar, walnuts, and cinnamon.

4. Roll dough into a 20×10-inch rectangle. Brush with melted butter; sprinkle with filling, leaving 1 inch unfilled along one long side. Roll up rectangle, starting from the filled long side; pinch dough to seal seams. Position roll, seam side down, and cut into eight slices. With slices on edges, snip or cut each slice, without cutting all the way through, into thirds. Place about 3 inches apart on the prepared baking sheet; spread each slightly to fan.

5. Cover; let rise in a warm place until nearly double in size (30 to 45 minutes). Preheat oven to 350°F. Bake 12 to 15 minutes or until golden. If desired, sift powdered sugar or drizzle with caramel ice cream topping over fantans. Serve warm. Makes 8 servings.

PER SERVING *348 cal., 13 g fat (6 g sat. fat), 48 mg chol., 388 mg sodium, 51 g carb., 2 g fiber, 20 g sugars, 7 g pro.*

CHERRY-COCONUT ANGEL ROLLS

CHERRY-COCONUT ANGEL ROLLS

PREP 30 minutes
CHILL 2 hours
RISE 1 hour
BAKE 30 minutes at 325°F
COOL 20 minutes

2½ cups all-purpose flour
1 pkg. quick-rise instant yeast
3 Tbsp. granulated sugar
1 tsp. salt
1 tsp. baking powder
½ tsp. baking soda
¼ cup cold, unsalted butter
¼ cup cold shortening, broken into pieces
1 cup buttermilk
 Nonstick cooking spray
¼ cup unsalted butter, melted
1 cup candied red cherries, chopped
½ cup chopped pecans, toasted (tip, page 49)
½ cup shredded coconut
 Coarse sugar (optional)
1 cup powdered sugar
½ tsp. vanilla
3 to 4 tsp. milk

1. Line the bottom of a 9-inch springform pan with parchment paper; set aside. In a large bowl whisk together flour, yeast, 3 tablespoons sugar, salt, baking powder, and baking soda.

2. Using a cheese grater, grate the cold butter over the flour mixture and toss to coat. Add shortening to flour mixture. Using your fingers, massage the butter and shortening into the flour mixture until it resembles coarse cornmeal.

3. Make a well in the center of the flour mixture; add the buttermilk. Using a wooden spoon, stir until the buttermilk is evenly distributed.

4. Transfer dough to a lightly floured surface. Knead 3 to 5 minutes or until smooth. Transfer to a large bowl coated with nonstick cooking spray; turn once to grease surface. Cover with plastic wrap. Chill 2 to 24 hours.

5. Turn dough out onto a lightly floured surface. Roll dough into a 15×12-inch rectangle; brush with melted butter. With a long side toward you, sprinkle cherries, pecans, and coconut over dough. Fold top and bottom thirds over filling. Pinch along the long open seam to seal.

6. Using a serrated knife coated with nonstick cooking spray, cut rectangle crosswise into 10 pieces. Arrange slices, cut sides up, in an even layer in prepared pan, folding each to form a U shape. Sprinkle with coarse sugar. Cover; let rise in warm place until double in size, about 1 hour.

7. Preheat oven to 325°F. Bake 30 to 35 minutes or until edges just start to brown and the center of rolls are cooked through. Cool in pan on a wire rack 20 minutes. Remove sides and bottom of pan.

8. In a small bowl combine powdered sugar and vanilla. Add enough milk to make glaze of drizzling consistency. Drizzle over rolls. Serve warm. Makes 10 servings.

PER SERVING 363 cal, 17 g fat (7 g sat. fat), 22 mg chol., 320 mg sodium, 50 g carb., 2 g fiber, 15 g sugars, 4 g pro.

BANANA PRALINE CRUNCH PULLAPART BREAD

PREP 25 minutes
RISE 1 hour 25 minutes
BAKE 45 minutes at 350°F
COOL 30 minutes

¾ cup milk
1 pkg. active dry yeast
1 egg, lightly beaten
¼ cup butter, melted
2 Tbsp. granulated sugar
½ tsp. salt
3 cups all-purpose flour
¼ cup butter, melted
1½ cups finely chopped bananas
¾ cup packed brown sugar
½ cup chopped, toasted pecans (tip, page 49)
1 tsp. ground cinnamon
1 recipe Coconut-Pecan Topping
2 oz. semisweet chocolate, melted

1. In a small saucepan heat the milk just until warm (105°F to 115°F). In a large bowl combine warm milk and yeast; stir until yeast is dissolved. Let stand 5 minutes.

2. Add egg, ¼ cup melted butter, sugar, and salt to yeast mixture. Beat with mixer on medium until combined. Add half the flour; beat on low 30 seconds, scraping bowl as needed. Beat 1 minute on medium. Stir in remaining flour. Shape dough into a ball (dough will not be smooth). Place dough in a greased bowl; turn once to grease surface. Cover and let rise in a warm place until nearly double in size (45 to 60 minutes).

3. Grease a 9×5-inch loaf pan. Turn dough out onto a lightly floured surface. Roll dough into a 20×12-inch rectangle. Brush with ¼ cup melted butter. Sprinkle with bananas, brown sugar, pecans, and cinnamon. Cut rectangle in half lengthwise to make two 20×6-inch strips. Cut each strip crosswise into five 6×4-inch strips. Carefully make two stacks of five strips each. Cut each stack into 4×2-inch pieces. Loosely stagger pieces in pan, cut sides up. Sprinkle with Coconut-Pecan Topping. Cover and let rise in a warm place until nearly double in size (40 to 45 minutes).

4. Preheat oven to 350°F. Bake 45 minutes or until golden brown (internal temperature should be 200°F). Cool in pan 10 minutes. Remove from pan to serving plate. Drizzle with melted chocolate. Cool 20 minutes more. Makes 10 servings.

Coconut-Pecan Topping In a medium bowl combine ¼ cup all-purpose flour, ¼ cup packed brown sugar, and ¼ teaspoon ground cinnamon. Cut in 2 tablespoons butter until mixture resembles coarse crumbs. Stir in 2 tablespoons flaked coconut and 2 tablespoons chopped pecans.

PER SERVING 464 cal, 20 g fat (10 g sat. fat), 51 mg chol., 236 mg sodium, 67 g carb., 3 g fiber, 32 g sugars, 7 g pro.

BANANA PRALINE
CRUNCH
PULLAPART BREAD

BABKA

BABKA

PREP 40 minutes
RISE 2 hours 15 minutes
BAKE 1 hour 10 minutes at 325°F

3	cups all-purpose flour
1	pkg. active dry yeast
¾	cup milk
½	cup butter, cut up
¼	cup sugar
1	tsp. salt
2	eggs
⅓	cup sugar
3	Tbsp. unsweetened cocoa powder
2	Tbsp. butter, melted
¾	cup miniature semisweet chocolate pieces
1	Tbsp. heavy cream

1. In a large bowl stir together 2 cups of the flour and the yeast; set aside. In a small saucepan heat and stir the milk, ½ cup butter, ¼ cup sugar, and salt until warm (120°F to 130°F) and butter is almost melted. Add to flour mixture along with one of the eggs. Stir until combined. Stir in as much of the remaining flour as you can.

2. Turn dough out onto a lightly floured surface. Knead in remaining flour to make a soft dough that is smooth and elastic (about 3 minutes). Shape dough into a ball. Place in a lightly greased bowl; turn once to grease surface of dough. Cover; let rise in a warm place until nearly double in size (1½ to 2 hours).

3. Punch dough down. Turn out onto a lightly floured surface. Cover and let rest 10 minutes. In a small bowl combine ⅓ cup sugar and the cocoa powder. Roll dough into a 16×12-inch rectangle. Brush with melted butter and sprinkle with cocoa mixture and chocolate pieces. Roll up rectangle, starting from a long side. Cut roll in half crosswise. Cut each piece lengthwise into thirds (some filling will fall out). For each loaf, braid three pieces together and sprinkle with some of the filling that falls out. Place each braid on a parchment-lined baking sheet. Cover and let rise in a warm place until nearly double (45 to 60 minutes).

4. Preheat oven to 325°F. Whisk together remaining egg and the cream. Brush over loaf. Bake 70 to 75 minutes or until golden and bread sounds hollow when gently tapped (internal temperature 180°F to 190°F), covering with foil the last 20 to 25 minutes to prevent overbrowning. Loosen loaf from pan and transfer to a wire rack to cool completely. Makes 12 servings.

PER SERVING *345 cal., 16 g fat (9 g sat. fat), 59 mg chol., 291 mg sodium, 46 g carb., 1 g fiber, 19 g sugars, 6 g pro.*

Make Ahead After shaping and placing in pan, cover and chill 24 hours. Let stand at room temperature 2 hours or until nearly double in size. Continue as directed.

CINNAMON ROLL WREATH

PREP 1 hour
RISE 2 hours 15 minutes
BAKE 25 minutes at 375°F
COOL 5 minutes

4½ to 5 cups all-purpose flour	
1	pkg. active dry yeast
1	cup milk
⅓	cup butter or margarine
⅓	cup granulated sugar
½	tsp. salt
3	eggs
¾	cup packed brown sugar
¼	cup all-purpose flour
1	Tbsp. ground cinnamon
½	cup butter or margarine
½	cup golden raisins
½	cup chopped pecans, toasted if desired (tip, page 49)
1	recipe Powdered Sugar Icing

1. In a large mixing bowl combine 2¼ cups of the flour and the yeast; set aside. In a small saucepan combine milk, the ⅓ cup butter, granulated sugar, and salt; heat and stir just until warm (120°F to 130°F) and butter is almost melted. Add to flour mixture. Add eggs. Beat with a mixer on low 30 seconds, scraping bowl constantly. Beat on high 3 minutes. Using a wooden spoon, stir in as much of the remaining flour as you can.

2. Turn dough out onto a lightly floured surface. Knead in enough of the remaining flour to make a moderately soft dough that is smooth and elastic (3 to 5 minutes total). Shape into a ball. Place in a greased bowl, turning once to grease the surface. Cover; let rise in a warm place until double in size (1½ to 1¾ hours).

3. Punch down dough. Turn out onto a lightly floured surface. Cover and let rest 10 minutes. Meanwhile, lightly grease a 13×9-inch baking pan; set aside.

4. For filling, in a small bowl combine brown sugar, the ¼ cup flour, and cinnamon. Using a pastry blender, cut in the ½ cup butter until mixture is crumbly.

5. Roll out dough into an 18×12-inch rectangle. Sprinkle filling over dough; top with raisins and pecans. Starting from a long side, roll dough into a spiral. Press seam to seal. Transfer dough to a large parchment-lined baking sheet. Shape spiral into a ring. With scissors snip almost to the center at 1-inch intervals. Pull sections apart and twist slightly, overlapping to shape a wreath. Seal ends together. Place a ramekin in the center of the wreath to help hold its shape while rising and baking.

6. Loosely cover; let dough rise in a warm place until nearly double in size (about 45 minutes).

7. Preheat oven to 375°F. Bake 25 minutes or until golden brown. Cool on a wire rack 5 minutes. Remove ramekin. Drizzle with Powdered Sugar Icing. Makes 16 servings.

Powdered Sugar Icing In a small bowl stir together 1¼ cups powdered sugar, ½ teaspoon vanilla, and enough milk (1 to 2 tablespoons) to make an icing of drizzling consistency.

PER SERVING *302 cal., 9 fat (6 g sat. fat), 48 mg chol., 146 mg sodium, 48 g carb., 1 g fiber, 35 g sugars, 5 g pro.*

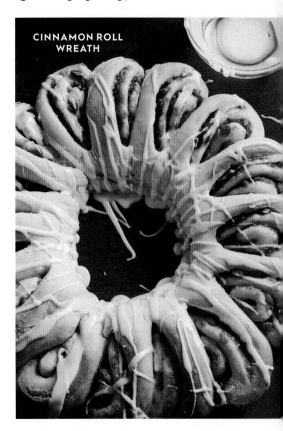

CINNAMON ROLL WREATH

MUESLI-HONEY BREAD

PREP 15 minutes
STAND 2 hours
RISE 45 minutes
BAKE 25 minutes at 450°F

1½ to 2 cups all-purpose flour
⅔ cup muesli
⅓ cup Add-Ins (optional)
1½ tsp. kosher salt
¾ tsp. active dry yeast
1 cup warm water (120°F to 130°F)
3½ Tbsp. honey
2 tsp. vegetable oil
  Cornmeal
  All-purpose flour

1. In a large bowl combine the flour, muesli, Add-Ins (if desired), salt, and yeast. In a glass measure stir together the water, honey, and oil; add to the flour mixture. Stir until moistened, adding more flour if necessary (dough will be very sticky and soft). Cover loosely with plastic wrap. Let stand at room temperature 2 hours.
2. Grease a baking sheet. Dust generously with cornmeal or flour. Do not punch dough down. Place dough on a well-floured surface; lightly flour top. Shape dough into a 14×3-inch loaf. Place dough on baking sheet. Sprinkle lightly with flour. Cover loosely with plastic wrap. Let rise in a warm place 45 minutes.
3. Preheat oven to 450°F. Using a sharp knife, score bread. Place on rack in center of oven. Place a shallow roasting pan with 2 cups hot tap water on the rack below. Bake 25 to 30 minutes or until crust is deep golden brown. Transfer loaf from pan to a wire rack; cool completely. Makes 10 servings.
Add-Ins Chopped Kalamata olives, snipped sun-dried tomatoes, chopped toasted nuts, snipped dried fruit, sliced green onions, shredded cheese, crumbled cooked bacon, or chopped pepperoni. (If using bacon or pepperoni, store bread in the refrigerator.)
PER SERVING *121 cal., 1 g fat (0 g sat. fat), 0 mg chol., 227 mg sodium, 25 g carb., 1 g fiber, 0 g sugars, 3 g pro.*

BITTERSWEET CHOCOLATE, HAZELNUT, AND MAPLE BACON SCONES

BITTERSWEET CHOCOLATE, HAZELNUT, AND MAPLE BACON SCONES

PREP 15 minutes
BAKE 12 minutes at 425°F
COOL 5 minutes

2   cups all-purpose flour
½   cup packed brown sugar
¼   cup unsweetened cocoa powder
2½ tsp. baking powder
½   tsp. baking soda
½   tsp. salt
½   cup cold butter, cut into 8 pieces
2   eggs
½   cup heavy cream
½   tsp. vanilla
¾   cup bittersweet or semisweet
     chocolate pieces
½   cup coarsely chopped hazelnuts,
     toasted (tip, page 101) or pecans,
     toasted (tip, page 49)
6   slices thick-sliced maple-flavor
     bacon, crisp-cooked and
     crumbled
     Coarse sugar, optional

1. Preheat oven to 425°F. In a large bowl stir together flour, brown sugar, cocoa powder, baking powder, baking soda, and salt. Using a pastry blender or your fingertips, cut or rub in the cold butter until mixture resembles coarse crumbs. Make a well in the center; set aside.

2. In a small bowl stir together eggs, ½ cup cream, and vanilla. Add egg mixture to flour mixture. Add chocolate pieces, hazelnuts, and bacon. Using a fork, stir just until moistened.

3. Turn dough out onto a lightly floured surface. Gently knead dough by folding and gently pressing 10 to 12 strokes or until nearly smooth. (Handle dough as little as possible to keep it light.) With a floured knife, cut dough in half. Lightly roll or pat each dough half into a 5½-inch circle. With a floured knife, cut each round into six wedges. Brush excess flour off tops of scones.

4. Place wedges about ½ inch apart on a parchment-lined or ungreased baking sheet. Brush scones with additional cream and, if desired, sprinkle with coarse sugar.

5. Bake 12 to 14 minutes or until bottoms are lightly browned. Remove scones from baking sheet. Cool on a wire rack 5 minutes. Serve warm. Makes 12 servings.

BOURBON PUMPKIN BREAD WITH SPICE SWIRL

PER SERVING *353 cal., 23 g fat (11 g sat. fat), 73 mg chol., 498 mg sodium, 33 g carb., 2 g fiber, 13 g sugars, 8 g pro.*

BOURBON PUMPKIN BREAD WITH SPICE SWIRL

PREP 25 minutes
BAKE 1 hour 5 minutes at 350°F
COOL 10 minutes

3⅔ cups sugar
1   cup finely chopped pecans
2½ tsp. pumpkin pie spice
3⅓ cups all-purpose flour
2   tsp. baking soda
1½ tsp. salt
1   15-oz. can pumpkin
4   eggs
1   cup vegetable oil
⅓   cup water
¼   cup bourbon or water
1   recipe Bourbon Icing (optional)

1. Preheat oven to 350°F. Grease bottoms and ½ inch up sides of two 9×5-inch loaf pans. In a small bowl combine ⅔ cup of the sugar, pecans, and 1½ teaspoons of the pumpkin pie spice. In an extra-large bowl stir together flour, baking soda, salt, and remaining pumpkin pie spice. Make a well in center of mixture.

2. In a large bowl combine remaining 3 cups sugar, pumpkin, eggs, oil, the water, and bourbon. Add all at once to flour mixture. Stir until combined. In each prepared pan spread half the batter; sprinkle with half the nut mixture.

3. Bake 65 to 70 minutes or until a toothpick inserted near center comes out clean; cover loosely with foil the last 15 minutes if needed to prevent overbrowning. Cool in pans on wire racks 10 minutes. Remove from pans; cool completely on wire racks. Wrap and store overnight before serving. If desired, drizzle with Bourbon Icing before serving. Makes 32 servings.

PER SERVING *238 cal., 10 g fat (1 g sat. fat), 23 mg chol., 198 mg sodium, 35 g carb., 1 g fiber, 24 g sugars, 3 g pro.*

Bourbon Icing In a small bowl stir together 1 cup powdered sugar, 1 tablespoon bourbon, and enough milk (2 to 3 teaspoons) to reach drizzling consistency.

CINNAMON-NUT BREAD

CINNAMON-NUT BREAD

PREP 30 minutes
BAKE 1 hour at 350°F
COOL 10 minutes

1½ cups sugar
⅔ cup finely chopped walnuts
2 tsp. ground cinnamon
2¼ cups all-purpose flour
1 tsp. baking powder
½ tsp. salt
1 egg
1 cup milk
⅓ cup vegetable oil
2 Tbsp. butter, melted

1. Preheat oven to 350°F. Grease and flour the bottom and ½ inch up the sides of a 9×5-inch loaf pan. In a small bowl stir together ½ cup of the sugar, the walnuts, and cinnamon.
2. In a large bowl stir together the remaining 1 cup sugar, 2 cups of the flour, the baking powder, and salt. In a medium bowl beat egg with a fork; stir in milk and oil. Add egg mixture all at once to flour mixture. Stir just until moistened (batter should be lumpy).
3. Spoon two-thirds of the batter into prepared pan. Sprinkle with half the walnut-sugar mixture. Using a thin metal spatula or table knife, cut down through batter and pull up in a circular motion to marble. Spoon remaining batter over top.
4. In a bowl combine the remaining walnut-sugar mixture and the remaining ¼ cup flour. Toss with the melted butter; sprinkle over batter in pan. Bake 60 to 65 minutes or until a toothpick inserted near center comes out clean. Cool in pan 10 minutes. Remove from pan, replacing any crumb topping that falls off. Cool on a wire rack. Makes 14 servings.
PER SERVING *268 cal., 11 g fat (2 g sat. fat), 19 mg chol., 145 mg sodium, 39 g carb., 1 g fiber, 23 g sugars, 4 g pro.*
Cranberry-Nut Bread Prepare as directed except fold 1 cup coarsely chopped cranberries into the batter.

**CHERRY-COCONUT
BANANA BREAD**

CHERRY-COCONUT
BANANA BREAD

PREP 25 minutes
BAKE 1 hour 5 minutes at 350°F
COOL 10 minutes

1⅓   cups all-purpose flour
½   cup oat flour
⅓   cup coconut flour
1½   tsp. baking powder
¾   tsp. ground ginger
½   tsp. baking soda
¼   tsp. salt
¼   tsp. ground nutmeg
2   eggs, lightly beaten
1½   cups mashed bananas (4 to 5)
1   cup sugar
½   cup coconut oil, melted
½   cup dried tart cherries, chopped
½   cup shredded coconut, toasted*
½   cup slivered almonds
2   Tbsp. flaxseed meal

1. Preheat oven to 350°F. Grease bottom and ½ inch up sides of a 9×5-inch loaf pan. In a large bowl combine the first eight ingredients (through nutmeg). Make a well in center of flour mixture.
2. In a medium bowl stir together eggs, bananas, sugar, and coconut oil. Add egg mixture all at once to flour mixture. Stir just until moistened (batter should be lumpy). Fold in cherries, ¼ cup of the coconut, ¼ cup of the almonds, and the flaxseed meal. Spoon batter into prepared pan.

Sprinkle with remaining coconut and almonds, pressing lightly.
3. Bake 65 to 70 minutes or until a toothpick inserted near center comes out clean. If necessary to prevent overbrowning, cover loosely with foil the last 15 minutes of baking. Cool loaf in pan 10 minutes. Remove from pan; cool on wire rack. Wrap and store overnight before slicing. Makes 12 servings.
*Tip To toast coconut, spread in a shallow pan. Bake in a 350°F oven 5 to 10 minutes, shaking the pan once or twice, watching closely to prevent burning.
PER SERVING *327 cal., 14 g fat (9 g sat. fat), 31 mg chol., 191 mg sodium, 45 g carb., 4 g fiber, 25 g sugars, 5 g pro.*

CHERRY AND
GOLDEN RAISIN
BREAD

CHERRY AND GOLDEN RAISIN BREAD

PREP 25 minutes
BAKE 1 hour at 350°F
COOL 10 minutes

2   cups all-purpose flour
1   cup sugar
2   tsp. baking powder
½   tsp. salt
¼   tsp. baking soda
1   egg
1   cup milk
⅓   cup cooking oil or melted butter
     or margarine
1   tsp. vanilla
½   cup coarsely chopped dried
     cherries or cranberries
½   cup golden raisins or coarsely
     chopped dried apricots
2   tsp. lemon zest
1   recipe Lemon Glaze

1. Preheat oven to 350°F. Grease the bottom and ½ inch up sides of an 8×4×2-inch loaf pan; set aside. In a large bowl stir together the flour, sugar, baking powder, salt, and baking soda; set aside.
2. In a medium bowl combine the egg, milk, oil, and vanilla. Stir in the cherries, golden raisins, and lemon zest. Add egg mixture all at once to flour mixture. Stir just until moistened (batter should be lumpy). Spoon batter into the prepared pan.
3. Bake 1 hour or until a toothpick inserted near center comes out clean. Cool in pan on a wire rack 10 minutes. Remove from pan. Cool completely. Wrap and store overnight at room temperature before serving.
4. Before serving, prepare Lemon Glaze. Drizzle glaze over loaf and sprinkle with additional lemon zest. Makes 16 servings.
Lemon Glaze In a small bowl combine ½ cup powdered sugar and 1 teaspoon lemon zest. Stir in enough lemon juice (1 to 2 teaspoons total) to make glaze of drizzling consistency.
PER SERVING *192 cal., 5 g fat (1 g sat. fat), 15 mg chol., 155 mg sodium, 34 g carb., 1 g fiber, 0 g sugars, 3 g pro.*

EASY BACON AND OLIVE FOCACCIA

EASY BACON AND OLIVE FOCACCIA

PREP 20 minutes
RISE 4 hours
BAKE 30 minutes at 400°F

1   cup millet flour or whole wheat flour
1   cup whole wheat flour
2   cups all-purpose flour
1   pkg. active dry yeast
2   tsp. kosher salt
2   cups warm water (120°F to 130°F)
     Nonstick cooking spray
8   slices bacon, chopped
1   Tbsp. olive oil
¾   cup whole, sliced, and/or chopped
     pitted olives

1. In large bowl combine millet flour, whole wheat flour, and 1 cup of the all-purpose flour. Stir in yeast and salt. Add the warm water. Stir until flour mixture is moistened (dough will be sticky and soft). Cover bowl; let stand at room temperature 2 hours.*

2. Grease a 15×10-inch baking pan. Stir the remaining 1 cup all-purpose flour into dough. Transfer dough to prepared baking pan. Using a rubber spatula coated with cooking spray, gently spread dough evenly in pan (dough will be sticky). Coat a piece of plastic wrap with cooking spray; cover dough with plastic wrap, coated side down. Let stand at room temperature 2 hours or until puffy.
3. Meanwhile, in a large skillet cook bacon just until starting to brown and still soft.
4. Preheat oven to 400°F. Using your fingertips, make indentations in surface of dough. Drizzle with oil. Top with bacon and olives. Bake, uncovered, 30 minutes or until golden brown. Cool slightly in pan on wire rack. Serve warm. Makes 12 servings.
PER SERVING *198 cal., 5 g fat (1 g sat. fat), 5 mg chol., 554 mg sodium, 31 g carb., 2 g fiber, 0 g sugars, 7 g pro.*
*Tip Or chill dough overnight. Let dough let stand at room temperature 30 minutes before continuing with Step 2.

DOUBLE-DECKER SKILLET GARLIC BREADSTICKS

PREP 15 minutes
BAKE 20 minutes at 400°F
STAND 5 minutes

Nonstick cooking spray
Cornmeal
5 Tbsp. butter, melted
2 cloves garlic, minced
1 tsp. dried oregano, crushed
½ tsp. black pepper
1 13.8-oz. pkg. refrigerated pizza dough
½ cup shredded mozzarella cheese (2 oz.)
¼ cup grated Parmesan cheese
2 Tbsp. snipped fresh parsley

1. Preheat oven to 400°F. Lightly coat a 10-inch cast-iron or other heavy oven-going skillet with cooking spray. Sprinkle lightly with cornmeal. In a small bowl combine melted butter, garlic, oregano, and pepper.

2. On a lightly floured surface, unroll pizza dough. Brush some of the butter mixture crosswise over half the dough; sprinkle with mozzarella cheese. Fold uncovered dough half over filling. Starting from folded edge, cut with a pizza cutter or sharp knife into 1-inch strips. Arrange strips in prepared skillet. Brush with remaining butter mixture; sprinkle with Parmesan cheese.

3. Bake 20 minutes or until golden. Let stand 5 minutes before serving. Sprinkle with parsley. Makes 9 servings.

PER SERVING 199 cal., 9 g fat (5 g sat. fat), 23 mg chol., 444 mg sodium, 23 g carb., 1 g fiber, 3 g sugars, 6 g pro.

BACON CORN BREAD

PREP 15 minutes
BAKE 20 minutes at 350°F

⅓ cup butter
¾ cup milk
2 eggs, lightly beaten
½ cup frozen whole kernel corn
1 cup yellow cornmeal
¾ cup all-purpose flour
⅓ cup sugar
1 Tbsp. baking powder
¾ tsp. salt
1 2.8- to 3-oz. pkg. cooked bacon pieces (⅔ cup)
¾ to 1 cup shredded cheddar cheese (3 to 4 oz.)

1. Preheat oven to 350°F. In an oven-safe 3½- or 4-quart nonstick Dutch oven*, melt butter over medium heat. Immediately remove pot from heat.

2. Add milk, eggs, and corn to butter in pot; stir to combine. Add the next five ingredients (through salt). Stir just until moistened (batter should be lumpy). Stir in half the bacon pieces and ½ cup of the cheese. Sprinkle remaining bacon and cheese over top.

3. Bake 20 to 25 minutes or until a toothpick inserted near center comes out clean. Serve warm. Makes 8 servings.

PER SERVING 327 cal., 16 g fat (8 g sat. fat), 87 mg chol., 865 mg sodium, 35 g carb., 1 g fiber, 10 g sugars, 12 g pro.

*Tip The diameter of the bottom of the Dutch oven should be 7½ to 8½ inches.

DOUBLE-DECKER SKILLET GARLIC BREADSTICKS

BACON CORN BREAD

Sweets for the Sweet

Find the perfect ending to holiday gatherings with these decadent desserts. Over-the-top cakes, updated pies, rich and creamy cheesecakes, and more are sweet reminders of the most wonderful time of the year.

CHOCOLATY PB&J
CHEESECAKE, PAGE 89

CRANBERRY-ROSEMARY
GALETTE, PAGE 90

ORANGE CORNMEAL CAKE

PREP 20 minutes
BAKE 45 minutes at 350°F
COOL 25 minutes

2   cups all-purpose flour
½   cup cornmeal
1½   tsp. baking powder
     Salt
¾   cup unsalted butter, softened

1¼   cups granulated sugar
4   eggs
1   cup whole milk
4   tsp. orange zest
2   tsp. vanilla
½   cup unsalted butter
⅓   cup packed brown sugar
1½   tsp. vanilla
1   Tbsp. fresh thyme leaves
1   large orange or 2 small oranges,
     sliced ⅛ inch thick

1. Preheat oven to 350°F. For batter, in a medium bowl stir together the flour, cornmeal, baking powder, and 1 teaspoon salt. In a large bowl beat the ¾ cup butter with a mixer on medium to high 30 seconds. Add granulated sugar. Beat 1 minute or until fluffy, scraping sides of bowl occasionally. Add eggs, one at a time, beating after each addition until combined. Alternately add the flour mixture and milk, beating on low after

ORANGE CORNMEAL CAKE

each addition just until combined. Stir in the orange zest and the 2 teaspoons vanilla; set aside.

2. Heat a 12-inch cast-iron skillet over medium heat 1 to 2 minutes. Add the ½ cup butter. Stir the butter around until melted and bottom of skillet is coated. Whisk in the brown sugar, 1½ teaspoons vanilla, and ⅛ teaspoon salt. Bring to boiling; boil 1 to 2 minutes or until thickened and caramelized. Stir in thyme leaves. Remove from heat. Lay orange slices in one even layer in the skillet. Spoon batter over oranges; spread evenly.

3. Bake 45 to 50 minutes or until top is golden and knife inserted near center comes out clean. Cool in skillet 5 minutes. Invert onto a serving plate; transfer any fruit stuck in skillet to cake. Cool 20 minutes. Sprinkle with thyme sprigs. Makes 8 servings.

PER SERVING *629 cal., 33 g fat (19 g sat. fat), 172 mg chol., 463 mg sodium, 76 g carb., 2 g fiber, 45 g sugars, 8 g pro.*

TRIPLE-LAYER COCONUT CAKE WITH LEMON CREAM

STAND 30 minutes
PREP 45 minutes
BAKE 15 minutes at 350°F
COOL 1 hour

4	eggs
2	cups all-purpose flour
2	tsp. baking powder
½	tsp. salt
2	cups sugar
1	cup unsweetened coconut milk*
¼	cup butter
2	tsp. vanilla
½	tsp. coconut extract (optional)
¾	cup flaked coconut, toasted (tip, page 73)
2	10-oz. jars lemon, lime, or orange curd
1	recipe Creamy Rich Frosting Fresh coconut curls** (optional)

1. Allow eggs to stand at room temperature 30 minutes. Meanwhile, grease and lightly flour three 9×1½-inch round cake pans; set aside. In a medium bowl stir together flour, baking powder, and salt; set aside.

2. Preheat oven to 350°F. In a large bowl beat eggs with a mixer on high 4 minutes or until thick and lemon color.

TRIPLE-LAYER COCONUT CAKE WITH LEMON CREAM

Gradually add sugar; beat on medium 4 to 5 minutes or until light and fluffy. Add flour mixture; beat on low to medium just until combined.

3. In a small saucepan cook and stir coconut milk and butter over medium heat until butter is melted. Stir in vanilla and, if desired, coconut extract. Add warm milk mixture to egg mixture; beat until combined. Stir in coconut. Spoon batter into prepared pans, spreading evenly.

4. Bake 15 to 18 minutes or until a wooden toothpick inserted near centers comes out clean. Cool cake layers in pans on wire racks 10 minutes. Remove layers from pans; cool completely on wire racks.

5. Place a cake layer, bottom side up, on a serving plate. Spread lemon curd on top of cake layer. Top with second cake layer, bottom side up. Spread lemon curd on second cake layer. Top with remaining cake layer, bottom side up. Spread top

and sides of cake with Creamy Rich Frosting. If desired, top with fresh coconut curls. Refrigerate leftovers. Makes 12 servings.

Creamy Rich Frosting In a large mixing bowl beat 1½ cups powdered sugar, 1 cup heavy cream, one 8-ounce carton sour cream, 1 teaspoon vanilla, and, if desired, ½ teaspoon lime, lemon, or orange zest with an electric mixer on medium until soft peaks form (tips curl). Makes 2⅔ cups.

PER SERVING *708 cal., 37 g fat (24 g sat. fat), 253 mg chol., 316 mg sodium, 89 g carb., 2 g fiber, 69 g sugars, 8 g pro.*

* Canned coconut milk separates in the can; stir well before measuring.

** To make fresh coconut curls, separate coconut meat from the shell in large pieces. Preheat oven to 350°F. Using a vegetable peeler, thinly slice coconut. Arrange slices on a baking sheet. Bake 3 to 5 minutes or just until edges start to brown and coconut is dry; cool.

PB&J LAYER CAKE

PREP 45 minutes
BAKE 30 minutes at 350°F
COOL 1 hour

- 2½ cups all-purpose flour
- 1 Tbsp. baking powder
- ½ tsp. salt
- ½ cup butter, softened
- ½ cup creamy peanut butter
- 2 cups granulated sugar
- 3 eggs, room temperature
- 2 tsp. vanilla
- 1¼ cups milk
- ¾ cup jam or jelly (any flavor)
- 1 recipe Creamy Peanut Butter Frosting

1. Preheat oven to 350°F. Lightly grease and flour three 8-inch round cake pans. In a medium bowl stir together flour, baking powder, and salt.

2. In a large bowl beat butter and peanut butter with a mixer on medium to high 30 seconds. Gradually add sugar, ¼ cup at a time, beating on medium until combined. Scrape bowl; beat 2 minutes more. Add eggs, one at a time, beating after each addition. Beat in vanilla. Alternately, add flour mixture and milk, beating on low after each addition just until combined. Spread batter into prepared pans.

3. Bake 30 to 35 minutes or until toothpick inserted near centers comes out clean. Cool cake layers in pans 15 minutes.

Remove layers from pans; cool completely on wire racks.

4. Place one cake layer on a platter. Spread with ¼ cup jam. Top with second layer, spread with ¼ cup jam, and top with third layer. Frost top and sides with Creamy Peanut Butter Frosting. Microwave remaining jam until smooth and thin enough to drizzle, stirring as needed. Drizzle melted jam over cake. Refrigerate leftovers. Makes 16 servings.

Creamy Peanut Butter Frosting In a large bowl beat one 8-ounce package cream cheese, softened; ⅔ cup creamy peanut butter; ¼ cup butter, softened; and 1 tablespoon vanilla with a mixer on medium until light and fluffy. Gradually beat in 6 cups powdered sugar. Beat in enough milk (2 to 3 tablespoons) to reach spreading consistency.

PER SERVING 651 cal., 25 g fat (11 g sat. fat), 74 mg chol., 386 mg sodium, 102 g carb., 2 g fiber, 80 g sugars, 9 g pro.

RED VELVET CAKE

STAND 30 minutes
PREP 45 minutes
BAKE 22 minutes at 350°F
COOL 1 hour

- 3 eggs
- ¾ cup butter
- 3 cups all-purpose flour
- 1 Tbsp. unsweetened cocoa powder
- ¾ tsp. salt
- 2¼ cups sugar
- 1 1-oz. bottle red food coloring (2 Tbsp.)
- 1½ tsp. vanilla
- 1½ cups buttermilk or sour milk*
- 1½ tsp. baking soda
- 1½ tsp. vinegar
- 1 recipe Creamy White Frosting Round peppermint candy, some broken

1. Allow eggs and butter to stand at room temperature 30 minutes. Meanwhile, grease and lightly flour three 8×2-inch round cake pans. In a medium bowl stir together flour, cocoa powder, and salt; set aside.

2. Preheat oven to 350°F. In an extra-large bowl beat butter with a mixer on medium to high 30 seconds. Gradually add sugar, about ¼ cup at a time, beating on medium until well mixed. Scrape sides of bowl; beat on medium 2 minutes more. Add eggs, one at a time, beating well after each addition. Beat in food

PB&J LAYER CAKE

coloring and vanilla. Alternately add flour mixture and buttermilk to egg mixture, beating on low after each addition just until combined. In a small bowl combine baking soda and vinegar; fold into batter. Spread batter into prepared pans.

3. Bake 22 to 25 minutes or until a toothpick inserted near centers comes out clean. Cool cake layers in pans on wire racks 10 minutes. Remove cake layers from pans; cool completely on wire racks.

4. Prepare Creamy White Frosting. To assemble, place one cake layer, bottom side up, on a serving platter. Spread with ¾ cup frosting; add another layer and spread with ¾ cup frosting. Add the remaining layer and spread top and sides with remaining frosting. Decorate top and bottom edge of cake with peppermint candy. Makes 16 servings.

Creamy White Frosting In a large bowl beat ½ cup shortening, ½ cup butter, 1½ teaspoons vanilla, and ½ teaspoon almond extract with a mixer on medium 30 seconds. Gradually add 2 cups powdered sugar, beating well. Add 2 tablespoons milk. Gradually beat in 2 cups powdered sugar. Gradually add 1 to 2 tablespoons milk until frosting reaches a spreading consistency. Makes about 3 cups.

PER SERVING *544 cal., 28 g fat (17 g sat. fat), 106 mg chol., 514 mg sodium, 70 g carb., 1 g fiber, 50 g sugars, 6 g pro.*

*Tip To make 1½ cups sour milk, place 4½ teaspoons lemon juice or vinegar in a glass measuring cup. Add enough milk to equal 1½ cups total liquid; stir. Let stand 5 minutes before using.

TOASTED BUTTER PECAN CAKE

PREP 35 minutes
BAKE 30 minutes at 350°F
COOL 10 minutes

- 1⅓ cups chopped pecans
- 3 Tbsp. butter, cut up
- 2 cups all-purpose flour
- 1½ tsp. baking powder
- ¼ tsp. salt
- ⅔ cup butter, softened
- 1½ cups sugar
- 2 eggs, room temperature
- 1½ tsp. vanilla
- 1 cup milk
- 1 recipe Vanilla Frosting

1. Preheat oven to 350°F. For buttered pecans, spread pecans in a shallow baking pan; dot with the 3 tablespoons butter. Bake 6 to 8 minutes or until toasted, stirring occasionally. Let cool.
2. Meanwhile, grease and lightly flour two 8-inch round cake pans. In a medium bowl stir together flour, baking powder, and salt.
3. In a large bowl beat the ⅔ cup butter with a mixer on medium to high 30 seconds. Gradually add sugar, ¼ cup at a time, beating on medium until well combined. Scrape sides of bowl; beat 2 minutes more. Add eggs, one at a time, beating well after each addition. Beat in vanilla. Add flour mixture and milk alternately, beating on low after each addition just until combined. Beat on medium to high 20 seconds more. Fold in 1 cup of the buttered pecans. Spread batter evenly into prepared pans.
4. Bake 30 to 35 minutes or until a toothpick comes out clean. Cool cake layers in pans on wire racks 10 minutes. Remove layers from pans; cool on wire racks. Frost with Vanilla Frosting. Decorate with remaining buttered pecans. Makes 12 servings.
Vanilla Frosting In a medium bowl beat ¼ cup softened butter and 1 teaspoon vanilla with a mixer on medium until light and fluffy. Gradually beat in 2 cups powdered sugar. Add 4 Tbsp. half-and-half. Gradually beat in an additional 2½ cups powdered sugar and an additional 1 to 2 tablespoons half-and-half until spreading consistency.
PER SERVING *615 cal, 28 g fat (12 g sat. fat), 80 mg chol., 271 mg sodium, 89 g carb., 2 g fiber, 71 g sugars, 5 g pro.*

RED VELVET CAKE ROLL

PREP 30 minutes
STAND 30 minutes
BAKE 12 minutes at 375°F
CHILL 1 hour

- 4 eggs
- ⅓ cup all-purpose flour
- 1 Tbsp. unsweetened cocoa powder
- 1 tsp. baking powder
- ½ tsp. vanilla
- ⅓ cup granulated sugar
- 1 Tbsp. red food coloring
- ½ cup granulated sugar

TOASTED BUTTER PECAN CAKE

RED VELVET CAKE ROLL

Powdered sugar
1 cup frozen light whipped dessert topping, thawed
½ cup light sour cream
½ tsp. vanilla

1. Separate eggs. Allow egg whites and yolks to stand at room temperature 30 minutes. Meanwhile, grease a 15×10×1-inch baking pan. Line bottom of pan with waxed paper or parchment paper; grease paper. Set pan aside. In a medium bowl stir together flour, cocoa powder, and baking powder; set aside.
2. Preheat oven to 375°F. In a medium bowl beat egg yolks and ½ teaspoon vanilla with a mixer on high 5 minutes or until thick and lemon color. Gradually add ⅓ cup granulated sugar, beating on high until sugar is almost dissolved. Beat in food coloring.
3. Thoroughly wash beaters. In another bowl beat egg whites on medium until soft peaks form (tips curl). Gradually add ½ cup granulated sugar, beating until stiff peaks form (tips stand straight). Fold egg yolk mixture into beaten egg whites. Sprinkle flour mixture over egg mixture; fold in gently just until combined. Spread batter in prepared baking pan.
4. Bake 12 to 15 minutes or until cake springs back when lightly touched. Immediately loosen edges of cake from pan and turn cake out onto a clean kitchen towel sprinkled with powdered sugar. Remove waxed paper. Roll towel and cake into a spiral, starting from a short side of the cake. Cool on a wire rack.
5. For filling, in a medium bowl fold together dessert topping, sour cream, and ½ teaspoon vanilla. Unroll cake; remove towel. Spread cake with filling to within 1 inch of the edges. Roll up cake; trim ends. Cover and chill up to 6 hours. Sprinkle cake with additional powdered sugar. Makes 10 servings.
PER SERVING *144 cal., 4 g fat (2 g sat. fat), 78 mg chol., 72 mg sodium, 24 g carb., 0 g fiber, 18 g sugars, 3 g pro.*

MARBLEOUS CHOCOLATE-PEANUT BUTTER CAKE WITH SALTED CARAMEL GLAZE

MARBLEOUS CHOCOLATE-PEANUT BUTTER CAKE WITH SALTED CARAMEL GLAZE

STAND 30 minutes
PREP 30 minutes
BAKE 40 minutes at 350°F
COOL 1 hour

2 eggs, room temperature
2 cups all-purpose flour
4 tsp. baking powder
½ tsp. baking soda
¼ tsp. salt
⅛ tsp. ground cinnamon
½ cup unsalted butter, softened
1¼ cups sugar
¾ cup sour cream
1 tsp. vanilla
⅓ cup milk
3 oz. bittersweet chocolate, melted and cooled
½ cup creamy peanut butter
1 recipe Salted Caramel Glaze
 Chopped peanuts (optional)
 Sea salt (optional)

1. Allow eggs to stand at room temperature 30 minutes. Grease a 10-inch fluted tube pan. Stir together flour, baking powder, baking soda, salt, and cinnamon.
2. Preheat oven to 350°F. In a large bowl beat butter with a mixer on medium 30 seconds. Gradually add sugar, about ¼ cup at a time, beating on medium until combined. Scrape bowl; beat 2 minutes more. Add eggs, one at a time, beating well after each addition. Beat in sour cream and vanilla. Alternately add flour mixture and milk, beating on low after each addition just until combined.
3. Transfer half the batter to a medium bowl; stir in melted chocolate. Stir peanut butter into the remaining batter.
4. Alternately drop spoonfuls of chocolate and peanut butter batters into prepared pan. Using a small metal spatula, swirl batters slightly to marble.
5. Bake 40 to 45 minutes or until a toothpick inserted near center comes out clean. Cool cake in pan 15 minutes. Remove cake from pan; cool completely on wire rack. Transfer to a serving plate. Drizzle cake with half the Salted Caramel Glaze. If desired, sprinkle with chopped peanuts and sea salt. Pass remaining glaze. Makes 12 servings.
Salted Caramel Glaze In a small heavy saucepan melt ¼ cup unsalted butter over medium-low heat. Stir in ¼ cup packed brown sugar and ¼ cup granulated sugar. Bring to boiling, stirring constantly. Stir in ½ cup heavy cream and return to boiling. Boil 2 minutes, stirring constantly. Remove from heat; stir in ½ to ¾ teaspoon sea salt. Cool completely.
PER SERVING *466 cal., 27 g fat (14 g sat. fat), 86 mg chol., 369 mg sodium, 53 g carb., 2 g fiber, 34 g sugars, 7 g pro.*

BLACK-AND-WHITE IRISH CREAM CUPCAKES

STAND 30 minutes
PREP 40 minutes
BAKE 20 minutes at 350°F
COOL 45 minutes

- ½ cup butter
- 4 egg whites
- 2 cups all-purpose flour
- 1 tsp. baking powder
- ½ tsp. baking soda
- ½ tsp. salt
- 1¾ cups sugar
- 3 Tbsp. Irish cream liqueur
- 1 tsp. vanilla
- 1¼ cups buttermilk or sour milk*
- 3 oz. bittersweet chocolate, melted and cooled
- 1 recipe Irish Cream Ganache
- 1 recipe Irish Cream Icing

1. Allow butter and egg whites to stand at room temperature 30 minutes. Meanwhile, line twenty-eight 2½-inch muffin cups with paper bake cups; set aside. In a medium bowl stir together flour, baking powder, baking soda, and salt; set aside.

2. Preheat oven to 350°F. In a large bowl beat butter with a mixer on medium to high 30 seconds. Add sugar, liqueur, and vanilla. Beat until combined, scraping sides of bowl occasionally. Add egg whites, one at a time, beating well after each addition. Alternately add flour mixture and buttermilk to butter mixture, beating on low after each addition just until combined.

3. Transfer about 2½ cups batter to a medium bowl; stir in melted chocolate. Fill each prepared muffin cup about two-thirds full, spooning chocolate batter into opposite side.

4. Bake 20 minutes or until tops spring back when lightly touched. Cool cupcakes in muffin cups on wire racks 5 minutes. Remove cupcakes from muffin cups. Cool completely on wire racks.

5. If desired, remove paper bake cups from cupcakes. Spread top of each cupcake with Irish Cream Ganache; add a small spoonful of Irish Cream Icing. Swirl slightly. Let stand until set. Makes 28 servings.

Irish Cream Ganache In a small saucepan bring ½ cup heavy cream just to boiling over medium-high heat.

Remove from heat. Add 6 ounces chopped bittersweet chocolate (do not stir). Let stand 5 minutes. Stir in 1 tablespoon Irish cream liqueur until smooth. Cool about 15 minutes or until slightly thickened. Makes about 1 cup.

Irish Cream Icing In a small bowl stir together 1 cup powdered sugar, 1 tablespoon Irish cream liqueur, and ¼ teaspoon vanilla. Makes about ½ cup.

PER SERVING 203 cal., 9 g fat (6 g sat. fat), 16 mg chol, 124 mg sodium, 30 g carb., 1 g fiber, 21 g sugars, 3 g pro.

***Tip** To make 1¼ cups sour milk, place 4 teaspoons lemon juice or vinegar in a glass measuring cup. Add enough milk to equal 1¼ cups total liquid; stir. Let stand 5 minutes before using.

CHALLAH, APRICOT, AND CARDAMOM BREAD PUDDING

PREP 20 minutes
BAKE 50 minutes at 350°F
COOL 10 minutes

- 4 cups dried challah bread cubes
- ½ cup dried snipped apricots
- ¼ cup chopped pistachios or pecans (optional)
- 2 eggs, lightly beaten
- 1¾ cups milk or eggnog
- ¼ cup butter, melted
- ½ cup granulated or packed brown sugar
- 1 tsp. ground cardamom
- 1 tsp. vanilla
  Heavy cream

1. Preheat oven to 350°F. Grease a 2-quart baking dish. Place bread cubes, dried apricots, and, if desired, pistachios in the dish. In a medium bowl whisk together eggs, milk, butter, sugar, cardamom, and vanilla. Pour over bread mixture in dish. Use a spatula to press bread down into the milk mixture.

2. Bake, uncovered, 50 minutes or until puffed and a knife inserted near the center comes out clean. Cool 10 minutes. Serve warm. If desired, drizzle with cream. Makes 8 servings.

PER SERVING 240 cal., 11 fat (6 g sat. fat), 86 mg chol., 138 mg sodium, 32 g carb., 1 g fiber, 22 g sugars, 6 g pro.

BLACK-AND-WHITE IRISH CREAM CUPCAKES

CHALLAH, APRICOT, AND
CARDAMOM BREAD PUDDING

CHOCOLATY PB&J
CHEESECAKE

CHOCOLATY PB&J CHEESECAKE

PREP 30 minutes
BAKE 50 minutes at 300°F
COOL 1 hour
CHILL 4 hours

- 1½ cups finely crushed chocolate wafer cookies or graham crackers
- ½ cup butter, melted
- 2 Tbsp. sugar
- 2 8-oz. pkg. cream cheese, softened
- 1 cup creamy peanut butter
- ¾ cup sugar
- 1 tsp. vanilla
- 4 eggs
- 1 cup miniature semisweet chocolate pieces
- ¾ cup strawberry or seedless raspberry jam or grape jelly
  Melted semisweet chocolate (optional)
  Fresh raspberries (optional)

1. Preheat oven to 300°F. For crust, in a medium bowl combine crushed cookies, melted butter, and the 2 tablespoons sugar. Press crumb mixture onto bottom and 1 inch up sides of a 9-inch springform pan. Place pan in a shallow baking pan.
2. In a large bowl beat cream cheese with a mixer on medium until smooth. Beat in peanut butter, the ¾ cup sugar, and the vanilla until combined. Beat in eggs, one at a time, beating on low after each addition. Stir in chocolate pieces. Spoon batter into prepared crust.
3. Bake about 50 minutes or until the outer 2 inches of the top is slightly puffed and looks dry (center will feel firm but may be darker).
4. Cool in pan on a wire rack 15 minutes. Using a small sharp knife, loosen crust from side of pan; cool 30 minutes. Remove side of springform pan; cool cheesecake completely on rack. Microwave jam 45 seconds or until smooth and thin enough to spread, stirring once. Spread jam over cheesecake. Cover loosely and chill at least 4 hours. If desired, top with fresh berries or drizzle with melted chocolate before serving. Makes 16 servings.
PER SERVING *475 cal., 31 g fat (14 g sat. fat), 90 mg chol., 297 mg sodium, 44 g carb., 1 g fiber, 33 g sugars, 8 g pro.*

BAKED APPLE DUMPLINGS WITH CARAMEL NUT FILLING

BAKED APPLE DUMPLINGS WITH CARAMEL NUT FILLING

PREP 35 minutes
BAKE 50 minutes at 375°F
COOL 30 minutes

- ¾ cup water
- ¾ cup sugar
- ½ tsp. ground cinnamon
- 2 Tbsp. butter
- 1 14.1-oz. pkg. rolled refrigerated unbaked piecrust (2 crusts)
- 4 small apples, such as Jazz, Empire, Granny Smith, Golden Delicious, or Idared
- 3 Tbsp. chunky peanut butter
- 2 Tbsp. caramel-flavor ice cream topping
- 2 Tbsp. finely chopped dried fruit, such as cranberries, tart red cherries, raisins, or apricots
- 1 egg

1. Preheat oven to 375°F. For sauce, in a small saucepan combine the water, sugar, and cinnamon. Bring to boiling; reduce heat. Simmer, uncovered, 5 minutes. Add butter; stir to melt. Pour sauce into a 2-quart square baking dish.
2. On a lightly floured surface, unfold one piecrust. Lightly brush with water. Place second piecrust on top of first. Roll into an 18-inch circle. Cut four 7-inch circles. If desired, use a small cookie cutter to cut shapes from scraps.
3. Core and peel the apples. Cut thin slices from bottoms so apples stand upright. In a small bowl combine peanut butter, caramel topping, and dried fruit. Fill apples with peanut butter mixture. For each dumpling, place a pastry circle on top of one apple and fold pastry over the apple, pleating at the bottom. Place dumplings on sauce in the baking dish. In a small bowl combine the egg and 1 tablespoon water. Brush tops and sides of dumplings with egg mixture. If using pastry cutouts, place on dumplings.
4. Bake, uncovered, 50 to 55 minutes or until apples are tender and pastry is golden. Cool 30 minutes. Spoon sauce over dumplings and serve warm. Makes 4 servings.
PER SERVING *675 cal., 30 g fat (12 g sat. fat), 69 mg chol., 521 mg sodium, 102 g carb., 4 g fiber, 60 g sugars, 6 g pro.*

PEAR FRANGIPANE CROSTADA

PREP 35 minutes
BAKE 40 minutes at 375°F

1   recipe Perfect Piecrust
4   oz. almond paste
2   eggs
4   tsp. cornstarch
⅛   tsp. salt
3   pears, cored and cut into ½-inch-thick slices
1   Tbsp. lemon juice
⅛   tsp. ground nutmeg
2   Tbsp. apricot preserves
¼   cup sliced almonds, toasted (tip, page 49)

1. Prepare Perfect Piecrust. Position rack in lower third of oven. Preheat oven to 375°F. In a food processor combine almond paste, one of the eggs, the cornstarch, and salt. Cover and process until well mixed. Dust a piece of parchment paper with flour. Place pastry on parchment. Using a rolling pin, roll crust into a circle 12 to 13 inches in diameter. Spread almond paste mixture in the center of crust leaving a 2-inch space around the edge.

2. In a large bowl toss pears with lemon juice and nutmeg. Arrange pears on top of almond paste mixture. Gently fold crust edge over pear mixture to just cover edges of pears, pleating as necessary. Transfer crostada on parchment paper to a baking sheet. In a small bowl beat the remaining one egg with a whisk; brush edge of crust with beaten egg.

3. Bake 40 minutes or until crust is deep golden brown and pears are soft. To prevent overbrowning, cover crostada loosely with foil the last 10 minutes of baking. Place apricot preserves in a small microwave-safe bowl. Microwave on high just until melted; brush over pears. Sprinkle with toasted almonds. Serve warm or cooled. Makes 6 servings.

Perfect Piecrust In a food processor combine 1¼ cups all-purpose flour, ¾ teaspoon sugar, and ½ teaspoon salt. Add ½ cup cold unsalted butter, cut into ½-inch pieces. Cover and pulse with several on/off turns until largest pieces are peasize. In a small bowl combine ¼ cup cold water and 1½ teaspoons white vinegar. Gradually pour vinegar mixture through feed tube into flour mixture in food processor (use only as much of the vinegar mixture as needed), pulsing with several on/off turns just until dough starts to form (mixture will appear dry but will form a soft dough when pressed with fingers). If dough still crumbles, pulse in a little more of the vinegar mixture. Turn out dough onto a sheet of plastic wrap. Quickly gather dough, kneading gently until it holds together. Form into a ball. Wrap in plastic wrap; press to flatten into a disk. Chill until ready to use (up to 2 days). Makes 1 single crust.
PER SERVING 444 cal., 25 g fat (9 g sat. fat), 101 mg chol., 273 mg sodium, 50 g carb., 5 g fiber, 20 g sugars, 8 g pro.

PEAR FRANGIPANE CROSTADA

CRANBERRY-ROSEMARY GALETTE
(PICTURED ON PAGE 79)

PREP 20 minutes
COOK 20 minutes
BAKE 45 minutes at 375°F

1   recipe Pastry for Single-Crust Pie (recipe, page 143)
1   large orange
3   cups fresh or frozen cranberries
¾   cup dried cranberries
¾   cup sugar
¾   cup cranberry juice
4   tsp. chopped fresh rosemary
½   cup chopped walnuts
     Milk (optional)
     Fresh rosemary leaves, snipped

1. Preheat oven to 375°F. Prepare pastry. On a large piece of lightly floured parchment paper, roll pastry to a 13-inch circle. Slide parchment and pastry onto a baking sheet. Set aside.

2. For filling, remove 1½ teaspoons zest and 6 tablespoons juice from orange. In a medium saucepan combine both cranberries, sugar, cranberry juice, and orange zest and juice. Bring to boiling; reduce heat. Simmer, uncovered, 20 to 25 minutes or until thickened. Remove from heat. Stir in chopped rosemary. Let cool slightly.

3. Spoon filling onto center of pastry, leaving 1½ inches border. Using parchment, lift and fold pastry edge over filling, pleating as necessary. Sprinkle filling with walnuts. If desired, brush pastry with milk.

4. Bake 45 minutes or until crust is golden. Cool slightly before serving. Top with rosemary leaves. Makes 6 servings.

PER SERVING *516 cal., 23 g fat (8 g sat. fat), 20 mg chol., 263 mg sodium, 76 g carb., 4 g fiber, 45 g sugars, 5 g pro.*

CINNAMON ROLL-SHINGLED SWEET POTATO PIE

PREP 35 minutes
BAKE 12 minutes at 450°F/55 minutes at 350°F

1   14.1-oz. pkg. rolled refrigerated unbaked piecrust (2 crusts)
1¼   lb. sweet potatoes, peeled and cut into 1-inch cubes
3   Tbsp. butter, melted
¼   cup granulated sugar
1½   tsp. ground cinnamon
2   eggs, lightly beaten
⅓   cup milk
⅓   cup sour cream
2   Tbsp. bourbon
1   tsp. vanilla
¾   cup packed brown sugar
2   Tbsp. all-purpose flour
¼   tsp. salt
¼   tsp. ground nutmeg

1. Let piecrusts stand at room temperature according to package directions. Meanwhile, in a large saucepan cook sweet potatoes in enough lightly salted boiling water to cover 15 minutes or until tender. Drain and return to saucepan. Use a potato masher to mash potatoes. Measure 1½ cups potatoes.

2. Place one piecrust on a lightly floured surface. Roll to a 14-inch circle. Brush with 1 tablespoon of the melted butter. In a small bowl combine granulated sugar and 1 teaspoon of the cinnamon. Sprinkle

CINNAMON ROLL-SHINGLED SWEET POTATO PIE

sugar-cinnamon mixture over pastry; press lightly with fingers. For topping, roll pastry into a log. Press to seal seam and ends. Cover and chill until needed.

3. Preheat oven to 450°F. Unroll remaining piecrust into a 9-inch pie plate. Fold under pastry even with edge of plate. Crimp edge as desired. Do not prick pastry. Line pastry with a double thickness of foil. Bake 8 minutes. Remove foil. Bake 4 to 5 minutes more or until set and dry. Remove from oven. Reduce oven temperature to 350°F.

4. In a large bowl whisk together eggs, milk, sour cream, bourbon, and vanilla. Stir in mashed sweet potatoes and the remaining 2 tablespoons melted butter. Stir in brown sugar, flour, remaining

½ teaspoon cinnamon, salt, and nutmeg until combined.

5. Pour sweet potato mixture into pastry shell. Cover edge of pie with foil to prevent overbrowning. Bake 30 minutes. Cut topping pastry log into ¼-inch slices. Remove pie from oven. Remove foil. Carefully arrange slices on filling close together without overlapping. Bake 25 minutes more or until filling is puffed and set and pastry is light brown. Cool on a wire rack. Cover and chill within 2 hours. Makes 8 servings.

PER SERVING *442 cal., 19 g fat (9 g sat. fat), 68 mg chol., 424 mg sodium, 64 g carb., 2 g fiber, 29 g sugars, 4 g pro.*

SPICED PEAR-
POMEGRANATE PAN PIE

APPLE CREAM CHEESE TURNOVERS

PREP 45 minutes
BAKE 15 minutes per batch at 400°F

3   Tbsp. butter
⅓   cup packed brown sugar
3   cups peeled, cored, and chopped Jazz, Granny Smith, or Jonagold apples
6   oz. cream cheese, cut up and softened
2   Tbsp. all-purpose flour
1   egg yolk
1   17.3-oz. pkg. frozen puff pastry sheets (2 sheets), thawed
1   egg, lightly beaten
1¼ cups powdered sugar
    Milk

1. Preheat oven to 400°F. Line two large baking sheets with parchment paper.
2. For filling, in a large skillet heat butter and brown sugar over medium heat until butter is melted. Add apples and ¼ cup water. Cover; cook 5 minutes. Uncover; cook 8 to 10 minutes more or just until apples are tender, stirring occasionally. Remove and cool slightly. Stir in 4 ounces of the cream cheese, the flour, and egg yolk; mix well.
3. On a lightly floured surface, unfold and roll out one pastry sheet to a 12-inch square. Cut into nine 4-inch squares. Spoon a rounded tablespoon of filling into the center of each square. Brush edges of pastry squares with water. Fold each pastry in half to form a triangle. Seal edges with the tines of a fork. In a small bowl combine the beaten egg and 1 tablespoon water. Brush half the egg mixture over pastries. Arrange on one prepared baking sheet. Bake 15 minutes or until puffed and golden. Cool on a wire rack placed over waxed paper. Repeat with remaining puff pastry, filling, and egg mixture to make nine more turnovers.
4. In a medium bowl beat the remaining 2 ounces cream cheese with a mixer on medium until smooth. Gradually beat in powdered sugar. Beat in enough milk, 1 tablespoon at a time, to reach a thick drizzling consistency. Spread turnovers with some icing. Sprinkle with cinnamon. Serve warm or cool. Makes 18 servings.
PER SERVING 225 cal., 12 g fat (7 g sat. fat), 35 mg chol., 145 mg sodium, 27 g carb., 1 g fiber, 15 g sugars, 3 g pro.

SPICED PEAR-POMEGRANATE PAN PIE

PREP 45 minutes
BAKE 55 minutes at 375°F

1   16.5-oz. tube refrigerated sugar cookie dough
⅔   cup all-purpose flour
1½ tsp. apple pie spice
    Nonstick cooking spray
2½ cups crushed gingersnaps
⅔   cup butter, melted
¾   cup granulated sugar
2   Tbsp. all-purpose flour
6   to 8 medium Bosc or d'Anjou pears, peeled, halved, cored, and thinly sliced
1   5.3-oz. container pomegranate seeds (about 1 cup)
2   tsp. vanilla
1   egg, lightly beaten
    Turbinado sugar or granulated sugar

1. Allow cookie dough to stand at room temperature 10 minutes. Preheat oven to 375°F. Place cookie dough in a bowl. Knead the ⅔ cup flour and ½ teaspoon of the apple pie spice into dough.
2. On a lightly floured surface, roll dough to ⅛-inch thickness. Using a variety of lightly floured leaf-shape cutters, cut dough into shapes, rerolling dough as needed.
3. Lightly coat a 15×10-inch baking pan with cooking spray. In a medium bowl toss together gingersnaps and melted butter. Press crumb mixture into bottom of prepared pan. Bake 5 minutes. Cool on a wire rack.
4. In a large bowl combine granulated sugar, the 2 tablespoons flour, and remaining 1 teaspoon apple pie spice. Add pears, pomegranate seeds, and vanilla. Toss gently to coat pears with sugar mixture. Add to crust-lined pan. Top with cutouts (small cutouts near center). Brush cutouts with lightly beaten egg; sprinkle with turbinado sugar.
5. Bake 30 minutes. Cover loosely with foil; bake 20 to 25 minutes more or until pear filling is bubbly and cookie leaves are golden brown. Cool on a wire rack. Makes 24 servings.
PER SERVING 242 cal., 10 g fat (4 g sat. fat), 16 mg chol., 153 mg sodium, 37 g carb., 2 g fiber, 21 g sugars, 2 g pro.

MAPLE-PUMPKIN
CRÈME BRÛLEE

MAPLE-PUMPKIN CRÈME BRÛLÉE

PREP 25 minutes
BAKE 40 minutes at 350°F
CHILL 4 hours
STAND 20 minutes

8   egg yolks
2   cups heavy cream
1   cup canned pumpkin
½   cup pure maple syrup
¼   cup packed brown sugar
2   tsp. vanilla
½   tsp. ground cinnamon
½   tsp. freshly grated nutmeg
⅓   cup granulated sugar

1. Preheat oven to 350°F. In a large bowl whisk together the first eight ingredients (through nutmeg). Spoon pumpkin mixture into eight 6-ounce ramekins or custard cups.
2. Place ramekins in a large roasting pan. Place roasting pan on oven rack. Pour enough boiling water into the roasting pan to reach halfway up the sides of the ramekins.
3. Bake 40 to 45 minutes or until edges are set (centers will shake slightly). Carefully remove ramekins from water; cool completely on a wire rack. Cover and chill 4 to 8 hours.
4. Before serving, let ramekins stand at room temperature 20 minutes. Meanwhile, in a medium-size heavy skillet heat granulated sugar over medium-high heat until sugar begins to melt, shaking skillet occasionally. Do not stir. Once sugar starts to melt, reduce heat to low and cook 5 minutes or until all sugar is melted and is golden, stirring as needed with a wooden spoon. Quickly drizzle the caramelized sugar over custards. (If sugar hardens in the skillet, return to heat; stir until melted.) Serve immediately. Makes 8 servings.
PER SERVING *386 cal., 27 g fat (16 g sat. fat), 292 mg chol., 36 mg sodium, 34 g carb., 1 g fiber, 28 g sugars, 4 g pro.*

EGGNOG SEMIFREDDO

EGGNOG SEMIFREDDO

PREP 45 minutes
STAND 30 minutes
FREEZE 6 hours

1   cup crushed gingersnap cookies (17 to 18)
3   Tbsp. butter, melted
3   eggs
2   egg yolks
¼   cup rum
1   cup superfine sugar
½   tsp. ground cinnamon
¼   tsp. freshly grated nutmeg
1½   cups heavy cream
      Freshly grated nutmeg (optional)

1. Line a 9×5-inch loaf pan with a double layer of plastic wrap, 2 inches extending on all sides. Set aside.
2. In a small bowl combine crushed gingersnap cookies and butter; toss together until cookie crumbs are moistened with butter. Evenly press mixture into the prepared loaf pan. Set aside.
3. In a large heatproof bowl combine eggs, egg yolks, and rum; stir in sugar, cinnamon, and nutmeg. Beat with a mixer on medium until combined. Place bowl over a saucepan filled with gently boiling water (upper bowl should not touch water). Cook, beating constantly on medium, until an instant-read thermometer inserted in center of mixture registers 140°F and maintains that temperature for 3½ minutes (15 to 18 minutes total). Remove from heat. Let stand at room temperature 30 minutes, stirring occasionally.
4. Wash beaters thoroughly; dry beaters. In another large bowl beat cream with a mixer on medium until soft peaks form (tips curl). Gently fold into egg mixture.
5. Carefully spoon mixture into crumb-lined loaf pan. Smooth surface. Cover pan tightly with plastic wrap. Freeze at least 6 hours or up to 3 days.
6. Remove plastic wrap from top of loaf pan. Using plastic wrap, lift semifreddo from pan; invert onto a chilled platter. Using a warm serrated knife, cut into slices. If desired, sprinkle slices with additional freshly grated nutmeg. Makes 8 servings.
PER SERVING *410 cal., 25 g fat (14 g sat. fat), 205 mg chol., 173 mg sodium, 38 g carb., 0 g fiber, 28 g sugars, 5 g pro.*

ALMOND SUGAR CUTOUT
COOKIES, PAGE 108

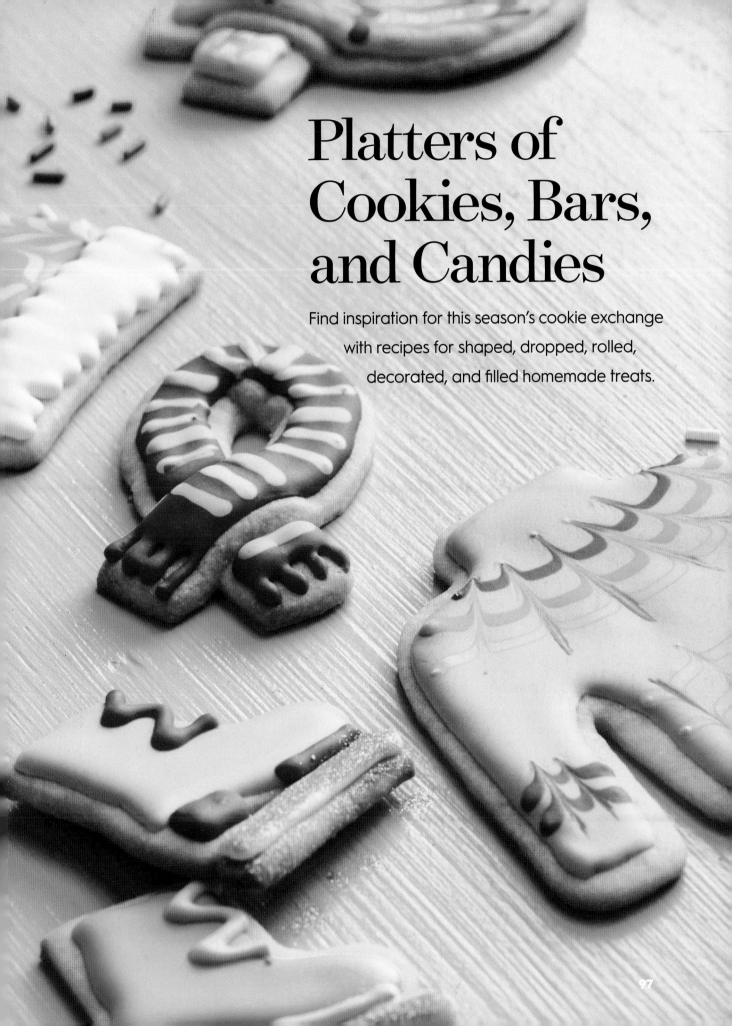

Platters of Cookies, Bars, and Candies

Find inspiration for this season's cookie exchange with recipes for shaped, dropped, rolled, decorated, and filled homemade treats.

SNOWBALL
TREES

SNOWBALL TREES

PREP 1 hour 10 minutes
BAKE 10 minutes per batch at 325°F
COOL 2 minutes

1   cup butter, softened
½   cup sugar
1   Tbsp. milk
1   tsp. vanilla
2¼ cups all-purpose flour
    Green paste food coloring
1   recipe Powdered Sugar Icing
    Decorative candies

1. In a large bowl beat butter with a mixer on medium to high 30 seconds. Add sugar. Beat until combined, scraping sides of bowl occasionally. Beat in milk and vanilla until combined. Beat in as much of the flour as you can with the mixer. Using a wooden spoon, stir in any remaining flour. Remove ½ cup of the dough. Tint the remaining dough with green food coloring.
2. Preheat oven to 325°F. For each cookie, use the green dough to shape ten ½-inch balls. For each tree, on an ungreased cookie sheet, arrange balls in a row of four, topped by a row of three, then two, then one on top. As you arrange the balls, gently press them into each other. Use the plain dough to make a ¾-inch ball and place it at bottom of tree for a trunk. Leave 2 inches between cookies on cookie sheet.
3. Bake 10 to 12 minutes or until edges are light brown. Cool on cookie sheet 2 minutes. Carefully transfer cookies to a wire rack; let cool.
4. Drizzle Powdered Sugar Icing across cookies to resemble strings of lights. Add decorative candies to icing for lights. Let stand until icing sets. Makes 36 cookies.
Powdered Sugar Icing In a medium bowl stir together 4 cups powdered sugar, 1 teaspoon vanilla, and enough milk (3 to 4 tablespoons) to make drizzling consistency.
PER COOKIE *141 cal., 5 g fat (3 g sat. fat), 14 mg chol., 37 mg sodium, 23 g carb., 0 g fiber, 16 g sugars, 1 g pro.*

MATCHA-GINGER SNOWBALLS

PREP 30 minutes
CHILL 1 hour
BAKE 10 minutes per batch at 350°F
COOL 2 minutes

½   cup shortening
1   Tbsp. grated fresh ginger or 2 tsp. ground ginger
1   Tbsp. vanilla
1   Tbsp. matcha (green tea powder)
1   tsp. lemon zest
1   cup packed brown sugar
1   tsp. baking powder
½   tsp. baking soda
¼   tsp. salt
2   eggs
2½ cups all-purpose flour
    Green food coloring (optional)
1   recipe Powdered Sugar Glaze
    White and gold nonpareils

1. In a large bowl beat shortening, ginger, vanilla, matcha, and lemon zest with a mixer on medium until combined. Add brown sugar; beat until fluffy. Beat in baking powder, baking soda, and salt. Beat in eggs. Beat in flour. If desired, beat in green food coloring. Chill dough 1 hour or until easy to handle.
2. Preheat oven to 350°F. Shape dough in 1-inch balls. Place balls 2 inches apart on ungreased cookie sheets. Bake 10 to 12 minutes or until lightly browned. Cool on cookie sheet 2 minutes. Remove; cool on wire racks.
3. Dip tops in Powdered Sugar Glaze, letting excess drip off, then sprinkle with nonpareils. Place cookies on waxed paper to dry. Makes 48 cookies.
Powdered Sugar Glaze In a medium bowl stir together 1½ cups powdered sugar and 2 tablespoons water until glaze is thick drizzling consistency.
PER COOKIE *87 cal., 3 g fat (1 g sat. fat), 8 mg chol., 40 mg sodium, 15 g carb., 0 g fiber, 9 g sugars, 1 g pro.*
To Store Layer cookies between sheets of waxed paper in an airtight container; cover. Store at room temperature up to 3 days or freeze up to 3 months.

CARAMEL-COFFEE SNICKERDOODLES

PREP 30 minutes
CHILL 1 hour
BAKE 10 minutes per batch at 375°F
COOL 2 minutes

1   cup butter, softened
1½ cups packed brown sugar
2   Tbsp. instant espresso coffee powder
1½ tsp. baking soda
1   tsp. cream of tartar
¼   tsp. salt
2   eggs
1   tsp. vanilla
¾   cup white whole wheat flour
½   cup amaranth flour
1½ cups all-purpose flour
¼   cup granulated sugar
2   tsp. ground cinnamon
20 vanilla caramels, unwrapped
3   Tbsp. half-and-half
1   tsp. instant espresso coffee powder

1. In a large bowl beat butter with a mixer on medium to high 30 seconds. Add the next five ingredients (through salt). Beat on medium 2 minutes, scraping bowl as needed. Beat in eggs and vanilla. Beat in whole wheat flour and amaranth flour. Beat in as much of the all-purpose flour as you can with the mixer. Stir in any remaining flour. Cover and chill about 1 hour or until dough is easy to handle.
2. Preheat oven to 375°F. In a small bowl combine granulated sugar and cinnamon. Shape dough into 1¼-inch balls. Roll balls in cinnamon-sugar to coat. Place balls 2 inches apart on an ungreased cookie sheet.
3. Bake 10 minutes or until bottoms are light brown. Cool on cookie sheet 2 minutes. Remove; cool on wire rack.
4. In a small saucepan heat caramels, half-and-half, and espresso powder over medium-low heat until melted and smooth, stirring frequently (or microwave 50 seconds, stirring twice). Drizzle over cooled cookies. Let cookies stand until caramel is set. Makes 42 cookies.
PER COOKIE *128 cal., 5 g fat (3 g sat. fat), 21 mg chol., 112 mg sodium, 19 g carb., 1 g fiber, 11 g sugars, 2 g pro.*

LINZERTORTE THUMBPRINT COOKIES

PREP 30 minutes
BAKE 14 minutes per batch at 325°F
COOL 2 minutes

⅓   cup toasted hazelnuts*
¼   cup powdered sugar
1   cup all-purpose flour
1½ tsp. unsweetened cocoa powder
½   tsp. ground cinnamon
⅛   tsp. ground cloves
½   cup butter, softened
2   tsp. lemon zest
⅓   cup seedless red raspberry jam or orange marmalade
    Powdered sugar (optional)
    Semisweet chocolate, melted (optional)

1. Preheat oven to 325°F. Line a large cookie sheet with parchment paper; set aside.
2. In a food processor combine hazelnuts and ¼ cup powdered sugar. Cover and process until nuts are finely ground. In a small bowl stir together flour, cocoa powder, cinnamon, and cloves. Set aside.

CARAMEL-COFFEE SNICKERDOODLES

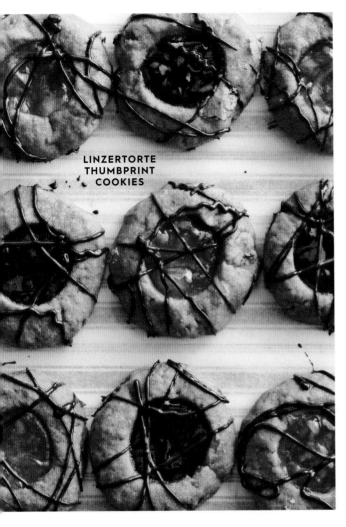

LINZERTORTE THUMBPRINT COOKIES

LEMON-CRANBERRY TASSIES

3. In a medium bowl beat butter and lemon zest with a mixer on medium to high 30 seconds. Add nut mixture; beat until combined. Beat in flour mixture.

4. Shape dough into 1-inch balls. Place 2 inches apart on prepared cookie sheet. Using your thumb, make an indentation in the center of each cookie.

5. Bake 8 minutes. Fill cookie centers with jam. Bake 6 to 8 minutes more or until bottoms are light golden brown. Transfer to a wire rack; cool. Sprinkle lightly with additional powdered sugar or drizzle with melted chocolate. Makes 16 cookies.

PER COOKIE *122 cal., 7 g fat (4 g sat. fat), 15 mg chol., 53 mg sodium, 13 g carb., 1 g fiber, 6 g sugars, 1 g pro.*

*Tip To toast hazelnuts, preheat oven to 350°F. Spread nuts in a shallow baking pan. Bake 8 to 10 minutes or until nuts are lightly toasted. Cool nuts slightly; place on a clean kitchen towel. Rub with towel to remove loose skins.

LEMON-CRANBERRY TASSIES

PREP 40 minutes
BAKE 10 minutes per batch at 350°F
COOL 5 minutes

½ cup shortening
1 cup packed brown sugar
1 Tbsp. vanilla
1 Tbsp. lemon zest
1 tsp. baking powder
½ tsp. baking soda
¼ tsp. salt
2 eggs
2½ cups all-purpose flour
¼ cup granulated sugar
1 cup purchased cranberry relish
   Sugared cranberries and fresh rosemary (optional)

1. Preheat oven to 350°F. In a large bowl beat shortening with a mixer on medium 30 seconds. Add brown sugar, vanilla, lemon zest, baking powder, baking soda, and salt; beat until combined. Beat in eggs until combined. Beat in flour.

2. Shape dough into 1-inch balls. Roll each ball in granulated sugar. Place each ball into a mini muffin cup; press into bottom and up the sides.

3. Bake 10 to 12 minutes or until golden. (If tassies puff during baking, repress with spoon.) Cool 5 minutes in cups. Remove; cool on a wire rack. Repeat with remaining dough. Fill cooled tassies with cranberry relish. If desired, top with sugared cranberries and rosemary leaves. Makes 36 cookies.

PER SERVING *108 cal., 3 g fat (1 g sat. fat), 10 mg chol., 56 mg sodium, 19 g carb., 0 g fiber, 8 g sugars, 1 g pro.*

Make Ahead Store unfilled tassies in an airtight container at room temperature up to 3 days or freeze up to 3 months. Fill just before serving.

PECAN-ORANGE CHOCOLATE CHUNK COOKIES

PECAN-ORANGE CHOCOLATE CHUNK COOKIES

PREP 30 minutes
BAKE 9 minutes per batch at 350°F

¾ cup butter, softened
1 cup packed brown sugar
½ cup granulated sugar
1 tsp. baking soda
½ tsp. salt
3 eggs
2 tsp. orange zest
1 tsp. vanilla
8 oz. unsweetened chocolate, melted and cooled
⅔ cup whole wheat flour
⅓ cup flaxseed meal
⅔ cup all-purpose flour
1 10- to 12-oz. pkg. semisweet chocolate chunks or dark chocolate pieces
⅔ cup chopped pecans, toasted (tip, page 49)

1. Preheat oven to 350°F. In a large bowl beat butter with a mixer on medium to high 30 seconds. Add both sugars, baking soda, and salt. Beat on medium 2 minutes, scraping bowl as needed. Beat in eggs, orange zest, and vanilla. Add melted chocolate; beat until combined. Beat in whole wheat flour and flaxmeal. Beat in as much of the all-purpose flour as you can with the mixer. Stir in any remaining flour. Stir in chocolate chunks and pecans.

2. Drop dough by tablespoons 2 inches apart onto ungreased cookie sheets. Bake 9 to 11 minutes or until puffed and tops are just set (do not overbake). Cool on cookie sheet 2 minutes. Remove; cool on wire racks. Makes 48 cookies.
PER COOKIE 140 cal., 9 g fat (5 g sat. fat), 19 mg chol., 81 mg sodium, 15 g carb., 2 g fiber, 10 g sugars, 2 g pro.

MAPLE-RAISIN OATMEAL COOKIES

PREP 30 minutes
BAKE 12 minutes per batch at 350°F

½ cup butter, softened
½ cup packed brown sugar
½ tsp. baking soda

- ¼ tsp. salt
- ⅓ cup pure maple syrup
- 1 egg
- 1½ tsp. vanilla
- ¾ cup all-purpose flour
- 1½ cups quick-cooking or regular rolled oats*
- ¾ cup raisins or dried cranberries
- 1 cup powdered sugar
- 3 Tbsp. pure maple syrup

1. Preheat oven to 350°F. In a large bowl beat butter with a mixer on medium 30 seconds. Add brown sugar, baking soda, and salt. Beat on medium 2 minutes, scraping bowl as needed. Beat in ⅓ cup maple syrup, egg, and 1 teaspoon of the vanilla. Beat in flour on low. Stir in oats and raisins.

2. Drop dough by teaspoons 2 inches apart onto an ungreased cookie sheet. Bake 12 minutes or until edges are set and centers are still soft. Cool 2 minutes on cookie sheet. Remove; cool on wire rack.

3. In a small bowl stir together powdered sugar, 3 tablespoons maple syrup, and remaining ½ teaspoon vanilla. If necessary, add milk or water, ½ teaspoon at a time, to reach desired consistency. Drizzle over cooled cookies. Makes 30 cookies.

PER SERVING *112 cal., 4 g fat (2 g sat. fat), 14 mg chol., 69 mg sodium, 20 g carb., 1 g fiber, 13 g sugars, 1 g pro.*

*Tip If using regular oats, use an additional ¼ cup all-purpose flour.

MINT-CHOCOLATE COOKIES

PREP 20 minutes
BAKE 8 minutes per batch at 350°F

- 1 17.5-oz. pkg. sugar cookie mix
- ½ cup butter, softened
- 1 egg
- ½ tsp. mint extract
- 4 oz. layered chocolate-mint candies, coarsely chopped, or 1 cup crème de menthe baking pieces
- 36 green candy coating disks or wafers*

1. Preheat oven to 350°F. Line a large cookie sheet with parchment paper; set aside.

2. In a large bowl stir together cookie mix, butter, egg, and mint extract until a soft dough forms. Stir in chopped chocolate-mint candies.

3. Drop dough by rounded teaspoons 2 inches apart onto prepared cookie sheet. Bake 8 to 10 minutes or until set.

4. Place a coating disk on top of each cookie. Cool cookies on cookie sheet 1 minute. Transfer to a wire rack; cool. Makes 36 cookies.

PER COOKIE *112 cal., 6 g fat (4 g sat. fat), 12 mg chol., 64 mg sodium, 15 g carb., 0 g fiber, 10 g sugars, 1 g pro.*

*Tip Look for green candy coating disks or wafers in the cake decorating section of hobby and crafts stores.

MAPLE-RAISIN OATMEAL COOKIES

MINT-CHOCOLATE COOKIES

SPEARMINT WHOOPIE PIES WITH WHITE CHOCOLATE-MASCARPONE FILLING

PREP 40 minutes
CHILL 30 minutes
BAKE 7 minutes per batch at 375°F
COOL 2 minutes

1   recipe White Chocolate-
    Mascarpone Filling
½   cup butter, softened
1   cup granulated sugar
½   tsp. baking soda
¼   tsp. salt
1   egg
1   tsp. vanilla
½   tsp. mint extract
2   cups all-purpose flour
½   cup buttermilk or sour milk
    (tip, page 86)
    Green food coloring
    Round striped spearmint candies,
    crushed (optional)

1. Prepare and chill White Chocolate-
Mascarpone Filling.
2. Meanwhile, in a large bowl beat
butter with a mixer on medium to high
30 seconds. Add sugar, baking soda, and
salt. Beat until combined, scraping sides of
bowl occasionally. Beat in egg, vanilla, and
mint extract until combined. Alternately
add flour and buttermilk to butter mixture,

beating on low after each addition just
until combined. Stir in desired amount of
green food coloring. Cover and chill 1 to
2 hours or until dough is easy to handle.
3. Preheat oven to 375°F. Line a cookie
sheet with parchment paper. Drop dough
by rounded teaspoons 2 inches apart
onto the prepared cookie sheet.
4. Bake 7 to 8 minutes or until edges
are set. Cool on cookie sheet 2 minutes.
Transfer cookies to a wire rack; cool.
5. Pipe or spread a thick layer of filling on
bottoms of half of the cookies. Top with the
remaining cookies, bottom sides down.
If desired, roll edges of whoopie pies in
crushed candies. Makes 36 whoopie pies.
White Chocolate-Mascarpone Filling In a
small heavy saucepan combine 3 ounces
chopped white baking chocolate with
cocoa butter and ¼ cup heavy cream.
Cook and stir over low heat until chocolate
is nearly melted. Remove from heat; stir
until smooth. Cool 15 minutes. Meanwhile,
in a large bowl beat ½ cup softened
mascarpone or cream cheese, and ¼ cup
softened butter with a mixer on medium
to high until smooth. Beat in ¼ teaspoon
vanilla. Gradually add 4 cups powdered
sugar; beat well. Beat in cooled white
chocolate mixture. Chill 30 minutes or until
firm enough to pipe.
PER WHOOPIE PIE *169 cal., 7 g fat
(4 g sat. fat), 22 mg chol., 78 mg sodium,
26 g carb., 0 g fiber, 20 g sugars, 1 g pro.*

GINGERBREAD MADELEINES

PREP 25 minutes
CHILL 2 hours
BAKE 10 minutes per batch at 375°F

½   cup butter, softened
½   cup granulated sugar
½   cup packed brown sugar
4   eggs
¼   cup molasses
1   cup all-purpose flour
½   cup cake flour
1   tsp. ground ginger
1   tsp. ground cinnamon
½   tsp. baking powder
¼   tsp. salt
¼   tsp. baking soda
¼   tsp. ground nutmeg
⅛   tsp. ground cloves
    Powdered sugar

1. In a large bowl beat butter with a mixer
on medium to high 30 seconds. Gradually
add granulated sugar and brown sugar.
Beat until light and fluffy, scraping sides
of bowl occasionally. Add eggs, one at
a time, beating well after each addition.
Beat in molasses until combined.
2. In a small bowl stir together all-purpose
flour, cake flour, ginger, cinnamon, baking
powder, salt, baking soda, nutmeg,
and cloves. Sprinkle about half the
flour mixture over the butter mixture;
fold in until combined. Repeat with the
remaining flour mixture. Cover and chill
batter 2 to 4 hours.
3. Preheat oven to 375°F. Grease and
flour twenty-four 3-inch madeleine molds.
Spoon batter into prepared molds, filling
each about half full.*
4. Bake 10 to 12 minutes or until edges are
golden and tops spring back when lightly
touched. Cool in molds 1 minute. Using the
point of a knife, loosen each madeleine
from the mold; invert mold over a wire
rack to release madeleines. Let cool. Dust
with powdered sugar before serving.
Makes 48 cookies.
PER COOKIE *61 cal., 2 g fat (1 g sat. fat),
21 mg chol., 48 mg sodium, 9 g carb.,
0 g fiber, 6 g sugars, 1 g pro.*
*Tip Let molds cool completely between
baking batches of madeleines. Grease
and flour molds for each batch.

SPEARMINT
WHOOPIE
PIES WITH WHITE
CHOCOLATE-
MASCARPONE
FILLING

GINGERBREAD MADELEINES

CITRUS SPRITZ

PREP 40 minutes
BAKE 6 minutes per batch at 375°F
STAND 20 minutes

¾ cup butter, softened
⅓ cup sour cream
⅔ cup granulated sugar
½ tsp. baking powder
¼ tsp. salt
1 egg
1 tsp. clementine zest
1 tsp. lemon zest
2½ cups all-purpose flour
⅓ cup finely ground slivered almonds
1 recipe Citrus Icing
   Yellow and/or orange sugar

1. Preheat oven to 375°F. In a large bowl beat butter with a mixer on medium to high 30 seconds. Beat in sour cream. Add granulated sugar, baking powder, and salt. Beat until combined, scraping bowl as needed. Beat in egg, clementine zest, and lemon zest. Beat in flour and ground almonds.
2. Force the unchilled dough through a cookie press 1 inch apart onto an ungreased cookie sheet. Bake 6 minutes or until edges are firm but not brown. Remove; cool on wire racks. Dip tops of cookies in citrus icing and sprinkle with yellow sugar. Let stand 20 minutes or until set. Makes 92 cookies.
Citrus Icing In a small bowl combine 2 cups powdered sugar and 1½ teaspoons clementine or lemon zest. Stir in 3 tablespoons clementine or lemon juice. If needed, stir in additional juice to make a thin coating consistency.
PER COOKIE *47 cal., 2 g fat (1 g sat. fat), 6 mg chol., 22 mg sodium, 7 g carb., 0 g fiber, 4 g sugars, 1 g pro.*

SNICKERDOODLE SHORTBREAD

PREP 15 minutes
BAKE 25 minutes at 325°F

1¼ cups all-purpose flour
6 Tbsp. granulated sugar
1 vanilla bean, halved lengthwise and seeds scraped, or 1 tsp. vanilla bean paste or extract*
½ tsp. ground cinnamon
½ cup butter, cut up

1. Preheat oven to 325°F. In a medium bowl combine flour, 3 tablespoons of the sugar, vanilla bean seeds, and ¼ teaspoon of the cinnamon. Add butter. Using a pastry blender, cut in butter until the mixture resembles fine crumbs and starts to cling together. Form the dough into a ball and knead until smooth.
2. In a small bowl combine remaining 3 tablespoons sugar and the remaining ¼ teaspoon cinnamon. On an ungreased cookie sheet pat or roll dough into an 8-inch circle. If desired, make a scalloped edge. Brush lightly with milk. Sprinkle generously with cinnamon-sugar. Cut into 16 wedges (do not separate wedges).
3. Bake 25 to 30 minutes or just until bottom starts to brown and center is set. While warm, recut circle into wedges. Cool on cookie sheet 5 minutes. Remove; cool on wire rack. Makes 16 cookies.
*Tip If using vanilla extract, drizzle over shortbread dough just before kneading.
PER COOKIES *106 cal., 6 g fat (4 g sat. fat), 15 mg chol., 46 mg sodium, 12 g carb., 0 g fiber, 5 g sugars, 1 g pro.*

PEANUT BUTTER-BROWNIE BISCOTTI

PREP 35 minutes
BAKE 20 minutes at 375°F/20 minutes at 325°F
COOL 1 hour

⅓ cup creamy peanut butter
¼ cup butter, softened
⅔ cup sugar
⅓ cup unsweetened cocoa powder
1½ tsp. baking powder
2 eggs
1 tsp. vanilla
1¾ cups all-purpose flour
1 cup chopped bittersweet or semisweet chocolate (about 6 oz.)
1 recipe Peanut Butter Icing

1. Preheat oven to 375°F. In a large bowl beat peanut butter and butter with a mixer on medium to high 30 seconds. Add sugar, cocoa powder, and baking powder. Beat until combined, scraping sides of bowl occasionally. Beat in eggs and vanilla until combined. Beat in as much of the flour as you can with the mixer. Using a wooden spoon, stir in any remaining flour and the chopped chocolate. If necessary, knead with your hands until dough comes together.
2. Divide dough in half. Shape each half into a 9-inch roll. Place rolls 3 inches apart on a large ungreased cookie sheet; flatten slightly until about 2 inches wide.
3. Bake 20 to 25 minutes or until a wooden toothpick inserted near centers comes out clean. Cool on cookie sheet on wire rack 1 hour.
4. Preheat oven to 325°F. Transfer baked loaves to a cutting board. Using a serrated knife, cut loaves into ½-inch slices. Place slices on cookie sheet. Bake 10 minutes. Turn slices over; bake 10 minutes more. Transfer to wire racks; cool. Dip tops of cookies into Peanut Butter Icing, using a narrow metal spatula to smooth the icing. Let stand until icing is set. Makes 32 biscotti.

Peanut Butter Icing In a small bowl stir together 1¼ cups powdered sugar, ⅓ cup peanut butter, and ¼ cup milk until smooth. Makes 1 cup.

PER BISCOTTI *138 cal., 7 g fat (3 g sat. fat), 16 mg chol., 66 mg sodium, 19 g carb., 1 g fiber, 11 g sugars, 3 g pro.*

PEANUT BUTTER-
BROWNIE BISCOTTI

PISTACHIO STAR SANDWICHES

PREP 30 minutes
CHILL 2 hours
BAKE 6 minutes per batch at 375°F

1 cup butter, softened
½ cup granulated sugar
¼ cup packed brown sugar
1 tsp. ground cinnamon
½ tsp. ground cardamom
¼ tsp. salt
1 egg
2 Tbsp. vanilla yogurt
2½ cups all-purpose flour
2 cups finely chopped pistachio nuts
1 egg white, lightly beaten
¼ cup butter, softened
2 cups powdered sugar
2 Tbsp. milk
1 tsp. vanilla

PISTACHIO STAR
SANDWICHES

1. In a large bowl beat the 1 cup butter with a mixer on medium to high 30 seconds. Add the next five ingredients (through salt). Beat until combined, scraping bowl occasionally. Beat in egg and yogurt. Beat in as much of the flour as you can with the mixer. Stir in any remaining flour and the pistachios. Divide dough in half. Cover and chill about 2 hours or until dough is easy to handle.
2. Preheat oven to 375°F. Lightly grease a cookie sheet. On a lightly floured surface, roll one portion of dough at a time to ⅛-inch thickness. Using a floured 3- to 3½-inch star-shape cookie cutter, cut out dough, rerolling scraps. Place cutouts on prepared cookie sheet. Using a small star-shape cookie cutter, cut and remove a star from centers of half the cookies. Brush cookies with egg white. Bake 6 to 8 minutes or until edges are light brown. Remove cookies; cool on a wire rack.
3. For filling, in a bowl beat the ¼ cup butter on medium until smooth. Add 1 cup of the powdered sugar, the milk, and vanilla. Beat on medium-high until smooth and creamy. Beat in enough remaining powdered sugar to reach spreading consistency.
4. Spread filling on bottoms of cookies without cutout centers. Top with cookies with cutout centers, bottom sides down. Makes 18 sandwich cookies.

PER SANDWICH COOKIE *358 cal., 20 fat (9 g sat. fat), 44 mg chol., 222 mg sodium, 40 g carb., 2 g fiber, 23 g sugars, 6 g pro.*
To Store Layer unfilled cookies between sheets of waxed paper in an airtight container; cover. Store at room temperature up to 3 days or freeze up to 3 months. Before serving, thaw cookies if frozen. Fill and assemble cookies.

ALMOND SUGAR CUTOUT COOKIES

PREP 35 minutes
CHILL 2 hours
BAKE 9 minutes per batch at 350°F

1 cup butter, softened
1½ cups sugar
½ tsp. baking powder
½ tsp. salt
2 eggs
2 Tbsp. milk
1 tsp. vanilla
½ tsp. almond extract
3 cups all-purpose flour
½ cup finely ground blanched almonds
1 recipe Royal Icing (optional)

1. In a large bowl beat butter with a mixer on medium 30 seconds. Add the next three ingredients (through salt). Beat until combined, scraping bowl as needed. Beat in the next four ingredients (through almond extract). Beat in flour and ground almonds. Divide dough in half. Cover and chill until easy to handle (about 2 hours).
2. Preheat oven to 350°F. On a lightly floured surface, roll one portion of dough at a time to ⅛- to ¼-inch thickness. Using a 3-inch cookie cutter, cut out dough. Place cutouts 1 inch apart on an ungreased cookie sheet.
3. Bake 9 minutes or until edges are firm and bottoms are very light brown. Remove; cool on a wire rack.
4. To decorate cookies as shown, make Royal Icing. Stir in additional warm water, about 1 teaspoon at a time, to make glazing consistency. Divide icing into small bowls and tint to desired colors. Fill disposable decorating bags with icing; snip one corner. To make knit designs in icing, spread one color icing onto a cookie. Working quickly, pipe contrasting colors in stripes on top of wet icing. Immediately pull a toothpick across the stripes to make a knit pattern. Let stand until set. Makes about 45 cookies.
PER COOKIE *105 cal., 5 g fat (3 g sat. fat), 20 mg chol., 73 mg sodium, 14 g carb., 0 g fiber, 7 g sugars, 1 g pro.*
Royal Icing In a large bowl stir together one 16-ounce package (about 4 cups) powdered sugar, 3 tablespoons meringue powder,* and ½ teaspoon cream of tartar. Add ½ cup warm water and 1 teaspoon vanilla. Beat with a mixer on low until combined. Beat on high 7 to 10 minutes or until stiff piping consistency. Use icing immediately or cover bowl with a damp paper towel; cover tightly with plastic wrap. Chill up to 48 hours. Makes about 5 cups.
***Tip** Look for meringue powder in the baking aisle of large supermarkets or in the cake decorating department of hobby and crafts stores.

ALMOND SUGAR
CUTOUT COOKIES

SNOWFLAKE
GINGERBREAD
SANDWICH
COOKIES

SNOWFLAKE GINGERBREAD SANDWICH COOKIES

PREP 35 minutes
CHILL 3 hours
BAKE 5 minutes per batch at 375°F

½   cup shortening
½   cup granulated sugar
1   tsp. baking powder
1   tsp. ground ginger
½   tsp. baking soda
½   tsp. ground cinnamon
½   tsp. ground cloves
½   cup molasses
1   egg
1   Tbsp. vinegar
2½   cups all-purpose flour
1   recipe Creamy White Frosting
     Coarse white decorating sugar

1. In a large bowl beat shortening with a mixer on medium to high 30 seconds. Add the next six ingredients (through cloves). Beat until combined, scraping sides of bowl occasionally. Beat in molasses, egg, and vinegar until combined. Beat in as much of the flour as you can with the mixer. Stir in any remaining flour. Divide dough in half. Cover; chill dough 3 hours or until easy to handle.
2. Preheat oven to 375°F. Grease a cookie sheet; set aside. On a lightly floured surface, roll half of the dough at a time to ⅛ to ¼ inch thick. Using a 2½- or 3½-inch snowflake-shape cookie cutter, cut out dough. Place 1 inch apart on prepared cookie sheet.
3. Bake 5 to 8 minutes or until bottoms are light brown. Cool on cookie sheet 1 minute. Transfer to a wire rack and let cool. Spread or pipe about 1 tablespoon frosting on the flat side (bottom) of half the cookies. Top with remaining cookies to make sandwiches.
4. Fill pastry bag fitted with a small round tip with Creamy White Frosting. Pipe snowflake design on cookie tops. Sprinkle immediately with coarse sugar. Makes 16 sandwich cookies.
Creamy White Frosting In a large bowl beat 1 cup shortening, 1½ teaspoons vanilla, and ½ teaspoon almond extract with a mixer on medium 30 seconds. Gradually add 2 cups powdered sugar, beating well. Add 2 tablespoons milk. Gradually beat in 2 cups powdered sugar. Gradually add 1 to 2 tablespoons milk until frosting reaches a spreading consistency.

COOKIES AND CREAM COOKIES

PER SANDWICH COOKIE *82 cal., 3 g fat (1 g sat. fat), 6 mg chol, 28 mg sodium, 13 g carb, 0 g fiber, 5 g sugars, 1 g pro.*

COOKIES AND CREAM COOKIES

PREP 30 minutes
CHILL 1 hour
BAKE 7 minutes per batch at 375°F

⅔   cup butter, softened
¾   cup granulated sugar
1   tsp. baking powder
¼   tsp. salt
1   egg
1   tsp. vanilla
2   cups all-purpose flour
1   cup crushed chocolate sandwich
     cookies with white filling (about
     10 cookies)

1. In a large bowl beat butter with a mixer on medium to high 30 seconds. Add sugar, baking powder, and salt. Beat until combined, scraping bowl as needed. Beat in egg and vanilla. Beat in as much of the flour as you can with the mixer. Stir in any remaining flour. Stir in ¾ cup of the crushed cookies. If necessary, cover and chill dough until easy to handle.
2. Shape dough into a 2-inch-diameter roll. Coat roll with the remaining ¼ cup crushed cookies. Wrap in plastic wrap or waxed paper; chill until firm enough to slice (1 to 2 hours in refrigerator or 30 minutes in freezer).
3. Preheat oven to 375°F. Use a serrated knife to cut roll into ¼-inch slices; place 2 inches apart on an ungreased cookie sheet.
4. Bake 7 to 9 minutes or until bottoms are lightly browned. Cool on cookie sheet 2 minutes. Remove; cool on wire rack. Makes 24 cookies.
PER COOKIE *133 cal., 6 g fat (4 g sat. fat), 21 mg chol, 108 mg sodium, 18 g carb, 0 g fiber, 8 g sugars, 2 g pro.*

ROSEMARY-WALNUT COOKIES

PREP 25 minutes
CHILL 1 hour
BAKE 7 minutes per batch at 375°F

⅔ cup butter, softened
¾ cup granulated sugar
1 Tbsp. finely chopped fresh rosemary
1 tsp. baking powder
½ tsp. freshly ground black pepper
¼ tsp. salt
1 egg
1 tsp. vanilla
2 cups all-purpose flour
⅔ cup finely chopped toasted walnuts (tip, page 49)

1. In a large bowl beat butter with a mixer on medium to high 30 seconds. Add the next five ingredients (through salt) and beat until combined, scraping bowl as needed. Beat in egg and vanilla. Beat in as much of the flour as you can with the mixer. Stir in any remaining flour. If necessary, cover and chill dough until easy to handle.

2. Divide dough in half. Shape each half into a 2-inch-diameter roll. Roll dough in chopped walnuts. Wrap each in plastic wrap or waxed paper; chill dough until firm enough to slice (1 to 2 hours in refrigerator or 30 minutes in freezer).

3. Preheat oven to 375°F. Use a serrated knife to cut rolls into ¼-inch slices; place 2 inches apart on an ungreased cookie sheet.

4. Bake 7 to 9 minutes or until bottoms are light brown. Cool on cookie sheet 2 minutes. Remove; cool on wire rack. Makes 24 cookies.

PER COOKIE *133 cal., 8 g fat (4 g sat. fat), 21 mg chol., 88 mg sodium, 15 g carb., 1 g fiber, 6 g sugars, 2 g pro.*

CONFETTI COOKIES

PREP 20 minutes
CHILL 1 hour
BAKE 7 minutes per batch at 375°F

1 pkg. 2-layer-size white cake mix
1 egg
½ cup butter, melted
½ cup red, white, and green sprinkles

1. In a large bowl stir together cake mix, egg, butter, and the sprinkles. Cover and chill dough 30 minutes* or until easy to handle.

2. Shape dough into a 2-inch-diameter roll. Wrap in plastic wrap or waxed paper; chill until firm enough to slice (30 to 60 minutes in refrigerator or 20 to 30 minutes in freezer).*

3. Preheat oven to 375°F. Use a serrated knife to cut rolls into ¼-inch slices; place 2 inches apart on an ungreased cookie sheet.

4. Bake 7 to 9 minutes or until bottoms are light brown. Cool on cookie sheet 2 minutes. Remove; cool on wire rack. Makes 24 cookies.

PER COOKIE *140 cal., 6 g fat (3 g sat. fat), 18 mg chol., 178 mg sodium, 20 g carb., 0 g fiber, 9 g sugars, 1 g pro.*

*Tip The length of time required for chilling will vary with the brand of cake mix.

ROSEMARY-WALNUT COOKIES

APPLE CRANBERRY CHEESECAKE BARS

PREP 25 minutes
BAKE 45 minutes at 350°F
COOL 1 hour
CHILL 4 hours

16   4½×2¼-inch graham cracker rectangles, finely crushed (2¼ cups)
½   cup butter, melted
¾   cup sugar
¼   tsp. salt
¼   tsp. ground cinnamon
2   medium Crispin, Piñata, Granny Smith, Pink Lady, and/or Empire apples, peeled, cored, and chopped
1   Tbsp. butter
2   8-oz. pkg. cream cheese, softened
3   eggs
1   tsp. vanilla
1   cup fresh or frozen cranberries

1. Preheat oven to 350°F. Line a 13×9-inch baking pan with foil, extending foil over edges of pan; grease foil.
2. In a medium bowl combine graham cracker crumbs, melted butter, 2 tablespoons of the sugar, salt, and cinnamon. Pat crumb mixture into prepared pan. Bake 10 minutes or until light golden brown. Cool on a wire rack.
3. Meanwhile, in a large skillet cook apples in 1 tablespoon hot butter 8 to 10 minutes or until tender, stirring occasionally.
4. For filling, in a large bowl beat cream cheese and remaining sugar with a mixer on medium until smooth. Beat in eggs and vanilla. Stir in cranberries and cooked apples. Pour filling over crust.
5. Bake 35 to 40 minutes or until set. Cool on a wire rack 1 hour. Cover and chill at least 4 hours. Using edges of foil, lift uncut bars out of pan. Cut into bars. Makes 24 bars.
PER BAR *188 cal., 12 g fat (7 g sat. fat), 54 mg chol., 170 mg sodium, 17 g carb., 1 g fiber, 11 g sugars, 3 g pro.*

APPLE CRANBERRY
CHEESECAKE
COOKIE BARS

KRUMKAKE

PREP 45 minutes
COOK 1 minute each

1⅓   cups all-purpose flour
¼   tsp. salt
¼   tsp. ground cardamom
3   eggs
1⅓   cups sugar
3   cups heavy cream
⅔   cup sour cream
2   tsp. vanilla
     Crushed peppermint candies
     (optional)

1. Grease and preheat krumkake iron press according to manufacturer's directions.
2. In a medium bowl whisk together flour, salt, and cardamom; set aside. In a large bowl beat eggs with a mixer on medium-high 3 minutes or until light in color. Gradually add 1 cup sugar, beating 2 to 3 minutes more or until thickened and lemon color. Alternately add flour mixture and 1 cup heavy cream to egg mixture, beating on low after each addition.
3. Spoon a rounded tablespoon of batter onto the iron press. Close; bake 1 minute or until brown. Remove; quickly roll around cone. Let cool 5 seconds; remove. Cool completely on wire racks.
4. For cream filling, in a large chilled bowl beat remaining 2 cups heavy cream, remaining ⅓ cup sugar, the sour cream, and vanilla on medium until stiff peaks form. Pipe or spoon into krumkakes just before serving. If desired, sprinkle with crushed peppermint candies. Makes about 36 cookies.
PER COOKIE *159 cal., 11 g fat (7 g sat. fat), 49 mg chol., 31 mg sodium, 12 g carb., 0 g fiber, 10 g sugars, 2 g pro.*

DOUBLE-ALMOND MACARONS

PREP 45 minutes
STAND 1 hour
BAKE 18 minutes at 300°F

3   egg whites
1¼   cups almond flour (such as
     Bob's Red Mill)
1¼   cups powdered sugar
⅛   tsp. cream of tartar
¼   cup granulated sugar
¼   tsp. almond extract
1   recipe Almond Butter Frosting

1. Place egg whites in a large mixing bowl and let stand at room temperature 30 minutes. Line two large cookie sheets with parchment paper; set aside.
2. Place the almond flour and powdered sugar in the bowl of a food processor. Cover and process 1 minute, stopping once to scrape up flour mixture from bottom of bowl. Sift the almond flour mixture, a little at a time, through a medium-mesh sieve into a medium bowl, pressing with the back of a spoon to pass through as much as possible. Discard any coarse almond flour that may be left in the sieve (up to 1 tablespoon).
3. Add cream of tartar to the egg whites. Beat with an electric mixer on medium until frothy, about 1 minute. Gradually add the granulated sugar and beat on high until stiff and shiny, about 4 minutes.
4. Gently add flour mixture to egg whites. Fold the flour mixture into egg whites by gently drawing a rubber spatula halfway through the mixture and fold until all flour mixture is incorporated, giving the bowl a quarter turn with each fold (about 50 strokes). Add the almond extract. Continue folding and turning, scraping down the bowl, until the batter is smooth and falls off the spatula in a thin flat ribbon, about 2 to 3 minutes. (You should have about 1½ cups batter.) Place ½ cup batter in each of two bowls. Tint one portion green and the other portion pink. (Leave one portion uncolored.)
5. Transfer batter (batter will be thin) to a large decorating bag fitted with a large (about ¼-inch) round tip. Pipe 1¼-inch circles 1 inch apart onto prepared cookie sheets. Firmly tap baking sheets five or six times against the counter to release air bubbles. Let stand 30 minutes or until cookies are no longer sticky to the touch.

KRUMKAKE

**DOUBLE-ALMOND
MACARONS**

6. Preheat oven to 300°F. Bake 18 minutes or until tops of cookies are set, shiny and rise ⅛-inch to form a "foot". Cool completely on cookie sheets on a wire rack. Carefully peel cookies off parchment paper.

7. Spread Almond Butter Frosting onto bottoms of half the cookies. Top with remaining cookies, bottom sides down. Makes 30 sandwich cookies.

Almond Butter Frosting In a medium bowl beat 3 tablespoons softened butter with a mixer on medium until smooth. Beat in 1 cup powdered sugar, 1 tablespoon milk, and ½ teaspoon almond extract until combined. Beat in 1 cup powdered sugar. If necessary, beat in milk, 1 teaspoon at a time, to reach spreading consistency. Makes 1 cup.

PER SANDWICH COOKIE 96 cal., 43 g fat (1 g sat. fat), 3 mg chol., 16 mg sodium, 16 g carb., 1 g fiber, 15 g sugars, 1 g pro.
To Store Layer filled cookies between sheets of waxed paper in an airtight container. Store at room temperature up to 3 days.

LACY FLORENTINES

LACY FLORENTINES

PREP 40 minutes
BAKE 8 minutes at 350°F

¾	cup sugar
½	cup butter
⅓	cup heavy cream
2	Tbsp. honey
1	cup quick-cooking rolled oats
1	cup finely chopped blanched almonds
½	cup finely chopped crystallized ginger
2	Tbsp. all-purpose flour
¼	tsp. lemon zest
4	oz. bittersweet, melted

1. Preheat oven to 350°F. Line two large cookie sheets with foil. Grease foil. In a medium-size heavy saucepan stir together the first four ingredients (through honey) over low heat until butter is melted and sugar is dissolved.
2. Bring to boiling over medium-high heat. To prevent sugar from crystallizing, brush sides of saucepan with a damp pastry brush or damp paper towel. Clip a candy thermometer to side of pan. Cook until thermometer registers 238°F (soft-ball stage). Remove from heat. Quickly stir in the next five ingredients (through lemon zest).
3. Drop dough by tablespoons 3 inches apart onto prepared cookie sheets. Flatten with a fork dipped in cold water.
4. Bake on separate racks 8 to 10 minutes or until light golden brown and set, rearranging sheets halfway through baking. Cool on cookie sheets. Gently remove from foil. Drizzle cookies with melted chocolate. Makes 36 cookies.
PER COOKIE *110 cal., 7 g fat (3 g sat. fat), 10 mg chol., 25 mg sodium, 12 g carb., 1 g fiber, 7 g sugars, 1 g pro.*

CRAN-MARNIER TRUFFLES

PREP 30 minutes
CHILL 2 hours

	Butter
1½	cups sugar
1	5-oz. can evaporated milk
½	cup butter
2	cups tiny marshmallows
8	oz. premium dark baking chocolate, chopped
1	Tbsp. Grand Marnier or other orange liqueur

CRAN-MARNIER TRUFFLES

GRAPEFRUIT GUMDROPS

2 tsp. orange zest
½ cup dried cranberries, finely snipped
12 oz. semisweet chocolate, chopped
2 Tbsp. shortening
Unsweetened cocoa powder (optional)

1. Butter the sides of a heavy 2-quart saucepan. In the saucepan combine sugar, evaporated milk, and the ½ cup butter. Cook and stir over medium-high heat until mixture comes to boiling. Reduce heat to medium; cook 6 minutes, stirring constantly. Remove from heat.
2. Add marshmallows, dark chocolate, liqueur, and orange zest; stir until melted and smooth. Stir in dried cranberries. Beat by hand 1 minute. Transfer mixture to a large bowl. Cover and chill 1½ hours or until nearly firm.
3. Line a cookie sheet with waxed paper. Shape chocolate mixture into 1-inch balls; place on prepared cookie sheet. Cover and chill 1 hour or until firm.
4. In a medium-size microwave-safe bowl microwave semisweet chocolate and shortening on medium 2 to 3 minutes or until melted and smooth, stirring after every minute. Cool slightly.
5. Dip balls, one at a time, into melted chocolate, letting excess drip back into bowl. Return chocolate-dipped balls

to cookie sheet. Chill 30 minutes or until chocolate is set. If desired, sprinkle truffles lightly with cocoa powder before serving. Makes 36 truffles.
PER TRUFFLE *110 cal., 6 g fat (3 g sat. fat), 6 mg chol., 23 mg sodium, 15 g carb., 1 g fiber, 13 g sugars, 1 g pro.*
To Store Place truffles, without cocoa powder topping, in a single layer in an airtight container; cover. Store in refrigerator up to 2 weeks. To serve, let stand at room temperature 30 minutes. If desired, sprinkle with cocoa powder.

GRAPEFRUIT GUMDROPS

PREP 30 minutes
STAND 2 hours

Nonstick cooking spray
1 cup granulated sugar
1 cup light-color corn syrup
1 grapefruit (1 tsp. zest, ¾ cup strained juice)
1 1.75-oz. pkg. regular powdered fruit pectin
½ tsp. baking soda
1 to 2 drops liquid red food coloring
½ cup coarse sugar

1. Line an 8×4×2-inch loaf pan with foil, extending foil over edges. Coat foil with nonstick cooking spray; set aside.

2. In a 1½-quart saucepan combine sugar and corn syrup. Bring to boiling over medium-high heat, stirring constantly to dissolve sugar. Reduce heat to medium; mixture should boil at a steady rate across surface. Cook without stirring 7 to 10 minutes or until a candy thermometer registers 280°F (soft-crack stage).
3. Meanwhile, in a 2-quart saucepan combine grapefruit juice, pectin, and baking soda. (Mixture will foam.) Bring to boiling over medium heat, stirring constantly. Remove; set aside.
4. Remove sugar mixture from heat; remove candy thermometer. Return pectin mixture to boiling. Gradually pour hot sugar mixture in a thin stream into boiling pectin mixture, stirring constantly. Cook 1 minute more, stirring constantly. Remove from heat; stir in zest and food coloring. Pour into prepared pan. Let stand at least 2 hours or until firm. Using foil edges, lift candy from pan. Cut into thirty-two 1-inch pieces. Store in an airtight container at room temperature up to 2 weeks or freeze up to 3 months. Just before serving or gifting, toss each piece in coarse sugar to coat. Makes 32 gumdrops.
PER GUMDROP *82 cal., 0 fat, 0 mg chol., 27 mg sodium, 20 g carb., 0 g fiber, 20 g sugars, 0 g pro.*

Thoughtful Food Gifts

Share gifts from your kitchen with friends, teachers, neighbors, and holiday party hosts. These prettily packaged homemade treats show thoughtfulness and caring.

to:

from:

COCONUT-CHERRY-
CHOCOLATE OATMEAL
COOKIES, PAGE 127

INDIVIDUAL BROWNIE
CHEESECAKES IN JARS,
PAGE 122

SPICED APPLE
TEA MIX

SPICED APPLE TEA MIX

START TO FINISH 15 minutes

- 2 Tbsp. loose green tea
- 2 Tbsp. snipped crystallized ginger
- 1 tsp. whole allspice
- 1 tsp. whole cloves
- 6 crisp dried apple chips* or dried apple slices
- 6 3-inch cinnamon sticks

1. For tea mix, in a bowl combine tea, crystallized ginger, allspice, and cloves.
2. Directions for serving: Add 6 to 8 ounces hot water to filled tea filter in each cup. Let tea steep 3 to 5 minutes. Remove and discard tea filter.
As a Gift Divide tea mixture and dried apple chips among six paper tea filters; tie closed with natural string embellished with a cinnamon stick. Place filled tea filters inside six decorative heat-proof cups. Make gift tags on brown craft paper. Trim and glue tags to red cardstock, making a ¼-inch border. Using a decorative clip, attach tags to paper cups suitable for hot beverages. Attach directions for serving. Makes 6 servings.
PER SERVING *2 cal., 0 fat, 0 mg chol., 5 mg sodium, 1 g carb., 0 g fiber, 0 g sugars, 0 g pro.*
***Tip** Look for dried apple chips with no added oils or sugar.

MEYER LEMON AND ROSEMARY MARMALADE

PREP 40 minutes
COOK 30 minutes
PROCESS 5 minutes

- 1½ lb. Meyer lemons (about 6 medium)
- 1½ cups water
- 2 Tbsp. snipped fresh rosemary
- ⅛ tsp. baking soda
- 5 cups sugar
- ½ 6-oz. pkg. liquid fruit pectin (1 foil pouch)

1. Score peel of each lemon into four lengthwise sections; remove the peels with your fingers. Using a sharp knife, scrape off and discard the white pith of peels. Cut peels into thin strips. Measure about 1½ cups peel strips.
2. In a medium saucepan combine the lemon peel strips, the water, rosemary, and baking soda. Bring to boiling; reduce

MEYER LEMON AND ROSEMARY MARMALADE

heat. Simmer, covered, 20 minutes. Do not drain.
3. Section lemons over a bowl, reserving juices; discard seeds. Add lemon sections and reserved juice to peels. Return to boiling; reduce heat. Simmer, covered, 10 minutes. Measure about 2½ cups lemon mixture.
4. In a 6- to 8-quart heavy pot combine the cooked lemon mixture and sugar. Bring to a full rolling boil, stirring constantly until sugar is dissolved. Quickly stir in pectin. Return to full rolling boil, stirring constantly. Boil hard 1 minute, stirring constantly. Remove from heat. Quickly skim off foam with a metal spoon, being careful not to remove peel.
5. Ladle hot marmalade into hot sterilized half-pint canning jars, leaving ¼-inch

headspace. Wipe jar rims; adjust lids and screw bands.
6. Process filled jars in a boiling-water canner 5 minutes (start timing when water returns to boiling). Remove jars from canner; cool on wire racks, turning and tilting jars after 20 minutes to distribute fruit evenly throughout marmalade. Repeat as necessary. (Do not invert sealed jars.) Makes 5 half-pints.
As a Gift Cover jar lid with a circle of printed or colorful fabric, tie with twine or colored string, and attach an herb-and-ornament embellishment.
PER SERVING *51 cal., 0 fat, 0 mg chol., 2 mg sodium, 14 g carb., 0 g fiber, 13 g sugars, 0 g pro.*

CINNAMON
POACHED
PEARS

PER SERVING *142 cal., 0 fat, 0 mg chol., 3 mg sodium, 33 g carb, 5 g fiber, 23 g sugars, 1 g pro.*

As a Gift Top a hinged jar with old-fashioned decorative bulb lights and festive pipe cleaners secured with hot glue.

Apple-Cranberry Poached Pears
Prepare as directed, except use 3 cups apple juice instead of wine and substitute 2 cups cranberry juice for the water. After chilling, transfer 2 cups syrup to a small saucepan. Bring to boiling; reduce heat. Simmer, uncovered, until syrup is reduced to ½ to ¾ cup. Spoon over pears.

INDIVIDUAL BROWNIE CHEESECAKES IN JARS

STAND 30 minutes
PREP 40 minutes
BAKE 15 minutes at 350°F
CHILL 4 hours

2	8-oz. pkg. cream cheese
2	eggs
	Nonstick cooking spray
12	vanilla wafers or chocolate sandwich cookies with white filling
2	oz. semisweet chocolate, chopped
¾	cup sugar
2	Tbsp. all-purpose flour
1	Tbsp. coffee liqueur or 1 tsp. vanilla
¼	cup milk
	Caramel-flavor ice cream topping
	Honey-roasted peanuts and/or caramel corn

1. Allow cream cheese and eggs to stand at room temperature 30 minutes. Meanwhile, coat twelve 4-ounce canning jars with cooking spray. Place a vanilla wafer in the bottom of each jar.
2. Preheat oven to 350°F. In a small saucepan cook and stir chocolate over low heat until melted; cool slightly. In a small bowl lightly beat eggs with a fork.
3. In a large bowl beat cream cheese with a mixer on medium to high 30 seconds. Add sugar, flour, and liqueur. Beat until combined. Stir in eggs and milk until combined. Transfer 1½ cups of the batter to a medium bowl; stir in melted chocolate.
4. Spoon plain batter into the prepared jars, filling each about half full. Spoon chocolate batter over plain batter, filling each jar nearly full. Place jars in a 13×9-inch baking pan. Place pan on oven rack. Pour enough boiling water into the baking pan to reach halfway up the sides of the jars.

CINNAMON POACHED PEARS

PREP 30 minutes
COOK 15 minutes
CHILL 2 hours

8	small to medium red and/or green pears (about 3 lb.)
1	750-ml. bottle dry white wine or 3 cups apple juice
2	cups water
1	cup sugar
1	2-inch piece peeled fresh ginger, cut into strips
1	3-inch piece stick cinnamon, broken
	Honey (optional)

1. Cut a thin slice from bottom of each pear so pears stand upright. Working through the bottom of each pear, use a melon baller to remove the core, leaving stem intact.
2. Meanwhile, in a 4-quart Dutch oven combine wine, the water, sugar, ginger, and cinnamon. Bring to a gentle boil over medium heat, stirring occasionally to dissolve sugar. Add pears. Return just to boiling; reduce heat. Simmer, covered, 15 minutes or just until pears are tender. Remove from heat; cool slightly.
3. Transfer pears and syrup to an extra-large bowl. Cover and chill 2 to 24 hours. To serve, drain pears. If desired, drizzle pears with honey. Makes 8 servings.

5. Bake 15 to 20 minutes or until puffed and set when gently shaken (cheesecakes will fall slightly as they cool). Carefully remove jars from water; cool on a wire rack. Cover and chill at least 4 hours.
6. To serve, top cheesecakes with caramel topping and sprinkle with peanuts and/or caramel corn. Makes 12 servings.

As a Gift Screw lids onto baked and cooled cheesecake jars. For a 2-jar snowman, cut off the toe from one baby sock and wrap the cut end with a length of twine. Glue tiny pom-poms to ends. Slide sock hat over top jar. Make a small cone-shape nose using a scrap of construction paper; glue to the top jar.

Stack to form a snowman. Adorn bottom jar with ribbon and pom-poms.
PER SERVING *305 cal., 19 g fat (9 g sat. fat), 73 mg chol., 191 mg sodium, 30 g carb., 1 g fiber, 24 g sugars, 5 g pro.*

INDIVIDUAL BROWNIE CHEESECAKES IN JARS

CHOW-DOWN SWEET AND SALTY SNACK MIX

START TO FINISH 20 minutes

- 7 cups bite-size corn square cereal and/or puffed corn cereal
- 2 cups pretzel sticks
- 1 cup salted peanuts
- ½ cup natural creamy peanut butter or peanut butter
- ½ cup semisweet chocolate pieces
- ½ cup dark chocolate pieces
- ¼ cup butter
- 1 tsp. vanilla
- 1⅓ cups powdered sugar

1. In an extra-large bowl combine cereal, pretzels, and peanuts; set aside. In a large microwave-safe bowl combine peanut butter, semisweet chocolate, dark chocolate, and butter. Microwave on high 30 to 60 seconds or until chocolate pieces are melted, stirring every 20 seconds.
2. Stir vanilla into chocolate mixture. Pour chocolate mixture over cereal mixture, stirring quickly to coat evenly.
3. In a 2-gallon resealable plastic bag combine cereal mixture and powdered sugar. Seal bag; shake to coat. Spread snack mix on a large sheet of parchment paper or foil; cool completely. Makes 18 servings.
PER SERVING *243 cal., 13 g fat (4 g sat. fat), 7 mg chol., 298 mg sodium, 30 g carb., 2 g fiber, 15 g sugars, 5 g pro.*

As a Gift Put snack mix in clear plastic bags; place inside one dog bowl. Top with a second bowl turned upside down. Tie bowls together with ribbon and embellish with a dog bone cookie cutter.

PEPPERMINT PENGUINS

PREP 40 minutes
BAKE 11 minutes per batch at 325°F

- 1 cup butter, softened
- ½ cup granulated sugar
- 1 Tbsp. milk
- 1 tsp. peppermint extract
- ¼ tsp. salt
- 2¼ cups all-purpose flour

CHOW-DOWN SWEET AND SALTY SNACK MIX

Orange and black paste food
colorings
White decorating icing

1. Preheat oven to 325°F. Line a cookie
sheet with parchment paper; set aside.
In a large mixing bowl beat butter with a
mixer on medium to high 30 seconds. Add
sugar, milk, peppermint extract, and salt.
Beat until combined, scraping sides of
bowl occasionally. Beat in as much of the
flour as you can with the mixer. Stir in any
remaining flour.
2. Remove ¾ cup of the dough and set
aside. Remove ⅓ cup of the dough and tint
with orange food coloring. Tint remaining
dough with black food coloring.
3. For each penguin, shape black dough
into one 1¼-inch ball and two ¼-inch
balls. Shape plain dough into one ¾-inch
ball. Shape orange dough into two
¼-inch balls and one ⅛-inch ball. On
the prepared cookie sheet, flatten the
1¼-inch black ball into a ¼-inch-thick
oval to make the body. For white tummy,
flatten the ¾-inch plain ball into a
¼-inch-thick oval. Place the tummy on the
body, bottoms of ovals aligned.
4. For wings, flatten the two ¼-inch black
balls to teardrop shapes. Position the
wings, rounded sides up, on each side of
the body above tummy. For feet, shape
the two ¼-inch orange balls into squares.
Using the handle of a spoon, make small
indentations in one side of squares for
webbed toes. Attach feet to the bottom
of body.
5. For beak, shape the ⅛-inch orange ball
into a triangle and position on body.
6. Bake 11 to 13 minutes or until edges
are set. Cool on cookie sheet 2 minutes.
Carefully transfer to a wire rack; cool.
Make eyes with dots of white icing, adding
dots of black food coloring for pupils. Let
stand until set. Makes 14 cookies.
PER COOKIE *240 cal., 13 g fat (8 g sat. fat),
35 mg chol., 159 mg sodium, 28 g carb.,
1 g fiber, 12 g sugars, 2 g pro.*
As a Gift Use a white paint pen and letter
stencils to write a greeting at the bottom
of a clipboard; let dry. Place cookies in a
clear 5×7-inch gift bag; secure under the
clip with a piece of 6×7-inch wrapping
paper beneath. Add festive ribbon trim.

PEPPERMINT
PENGUINS

LEMON-LAVENDER COOKIES

PREP 40 minutes
CHILL 2 hours
BAKE 10 minutes per batch at 350°F

1½ cups all-purpose flour
1   tsp. dried lavender buds, finely crushed
1   tsp. lemon zest
¼   tsp. salt
¾   cup butter, softened
1   cup powdered sugar
¼   cup butter, softened
1   Tbsp. milk
1   cup powdered sugar
     Milk (optional)
     Dried lavender buds (optional)
     Thin lemon peel strips (optional)

1. In a medium bowl stir together flour, crushed lavender buds, lemon zest, and salt; set aside. In a large mixing bowl beat ¾ cup butter with a mixer on medium to high 30 seconds. Add 1 cup powdered sugar. Beat until combined, scraping sides of bowl occasionally. Beat in as much of the flour mixture as you can with the mixer. Stir in any remaining flour mixture.
2. On a lightly floured surface, shape dough into a 10-inch log. Wrap log in plastic wrap or waxed paper. Chill 2 to 24 hours or until dough is firm enough to slice.
3. Preheat oven to 350°F. Cut roll into ¼-inch slices. Place slices 2 inches apart on an ungreased cookie sheet. Bake 10 minutes or until edges are light brown. Transfer cookies to a wire rack; cool.
4. For frosting, in a small bowl combine ¼ cup butter and 1 tablespoon milk. Beat in 1 cup powdered sugar until smooth. If necessary, stir in additional milk, 1 teaspoon at a time, to reach spreading consistency.
5. Spread cookies with frosting. If desired, top with additional lavender buds and lemon zest. Makes about 40 cookies.
PER COOKIE *91 cal., 5 g fat (3 g sat. fat), 14 mg chol., 62 mg sodium, 11 g carb., 0 g fiber, 7 g sugars, 1 g pro.*
As a Gift Roll a 12-inch length of corrugated cardboard to create into a 3-inch-diameter tube, allowing ½-inch overlap. Cut cork drink coasters to fit each end and hot-glue in place. Line interior with tissue paper, then nestle a stack of cookies in the tube. Wrap ribbon around cookie tube and insert a berry stem.

LEMON-LAVENDER COOKIES

COCONUT-CHERRY-CHOCOLATE OATMEAL COOKIES

PREP 40 minutes
BAKE 10 minutes per batch at 350°F
STAND 3 minutes

½   cup butter, softened
1   cup packed brown sugar
⅔   cup granulated sugar
2   tsp. ground cinnamon
1   tsp. baking soda
¼   tsp. salt
2   eggs
2   tsp. vanilla
1½   cups all-purpose flour
1½   cups rolled oats
1   cup flaked coconut
4   oz. dark chocolate, finely chopped
½   cup dried cherries or cranberries, chopped
½   cup walnuts, toasted (tip, page 49) and chopped

1. Preheat oven to 350°F. In a medium bowl beat butter with a mixer on medium to high 30 seconds. Add brown sugar, granulated sugar, cinnamon, baking soda, and salt. Beat until combined, scraping sides of bowl occasionally. Beat in eggs and vanilla until combined. Beat in flour just until combined. Stir in oats, coconut, chocolate, dried cherries, and walnuts.

2. Drop dough by a ⅓-cup measure onto an ungreased cookie sheet. Press dough mounds into 3½-inch rounds, leaving about 3 inches between rounds. Bake 10 minutes or just until edges are lightly browned and set. Cool on cookie sheet 3 minutes. Transfer to a wire rack; cool completely. Store between sheets of waxed paper in an airtight container at room temperature up to 3 days or freeze up to 3 months. Makes 16 cookies.

PER COOKIE *353 cal., 15 g fat (8 g sat. fat), 39 mg chol., 196 mg sodium, 52 g carb., 3 g fiber, 30 g sugars, 6 g pro.*

As a Gift Cut two rectangles of waxed paper just smaller than the width and overall length of a 5×5-inch envelope. Use a grater or crayon sharpener to shred green and yellow crayons into two separate piles. Lay a scrap of fabric on an ironing board; lay a piece of waxed paper on top. Sprinkle the shavings on the paper in the general shape of a tree. Place the second sheet of waxed paper on top, then add another scrap of fabric (fabric should be larger than waxed paper to protect ironing board from crayon). With iron on lowest heat setting, iron a few seconds to melt. Let cool, then use a crafts knife to cut a tree shape from the front of the envelope. Insert waxed paper, add a wrapped cookie, and fold down flap.

COCONUT-CHERRY-CHOCOLATE OATMEAL COOKIES

FUDGY CUT-OUT
BROWNIES

FUDGY CUT-OUT BROWNIES

PREP 20 minutes
BAKE 30 minutes at 350°F

½   cup butter
3   oz. unsweetened chocolate, coarsely chopped
1   cup sugar
2   eggs
1   tsp. vanilla
⅔   cup all-purpose flour
¼   tsp. baking soda
½   cup chopped nuts (optional)
1   recipe Chocolate-Cream Cheese Frosting (optional)

1. In a medium saucepan stir butter and unsweetened chocolate over low heat until melted and smooth; cool. Preheat oven to 350°F. Line an 8×8-inch baking pan with foil, extending foil over edges of pan. Grease foil; set pan aside.

2. Stir sugar into the cooled chocolate mixture. Add eggs, one at a time, beating with a wooden spoon after each addition just until combined. Stir in vanilla. In a small bowl stir together flour and baking soda. Add flour mixture to chocolate mixture; stir just until combined. If desired, stir in nuts. Spread batter in prepared baking pan.

3. Bake 30 minutes. Cool in pan on a wire rack. Makes 16 servings.

PER SERVING 157 cal., 10 g fat (6 g sat. fat), 43 mg chol., 90 mg sodium, 18 g carb., 1 g fiber, 12 g sugars, 2 g pro.

Chocolate-Cream Cheese Frosting In a small saucepan heat 1 cup semisweet chocolate pieces over low heat until melted and smooth; cool. In a medium bowl combine two 3-ounce packages softened cream cheese and ½ cup powdered sugar. Stir in melted chocolate.

As a Gift Paint the sides of a tin lid (extra-large rectangular tin with silver window) with white paint and sprinkle with clear glitter. Paint icicles on window and sprinkle with more glitter while wet; shake off excess. Cut out snowflake shapes from folded paper. Adorn the tin with snowflakes and pom-poms. Remove brownies from pan and place in tin. Top with cookie cutters. Include holiday sprinkles in cellophane bags tied with red-and-white bakers twine and a container of Chocolate-Cream-Cheese Frosting.

TRIPLE-BERRY PIE

PREP 30 minutes
BAKE 1 hour 5 minutes at 375°F

½   cup granulated sugar
¼   cup cornstarch
4   tsp. lemon zest
1   Tbsp. lemon juice
⅛   tsp. salt
2   cups fresh or frozen blackberries
2   cups fresh or frozen blueberries
2   cups fresh or frozen cranberries
1   recipe Pastry for Double-Crust Pie
1   egg, lightly beaten
1   tsp. water
3   Tbsp. turbinado (raw) sugar
½   cup heavy cream
¼   cup lemon curd

1. In a large bowl stir together granulated sugar, cornstarch, 2 teaspoons of the lemon zest, the lemon juice, and salt. Add blackberries, blueberries, and cranberries; toss gently to coat. (If using frozen berries, let mixture stand 30 to 45 minutes or until berries are partially thawed but still icy.)

2. Preheat oven to 375°F. Prepare Pastry for a Double-Crust Pie, except stir the remaining 2 teaspoons lemon zest into flour mixture with salt. On a lightly floured surface, use your hands to slightly flatten one pastry ball. Roll pastry from center to edges into a circle about 12 inches in diameter. Wrap pastry circle around the rolling pin. Unroll pastry into a 9-inch pie plate. Ease pastry into pie plate without stretching it. Transfer berry filling to pastry-lined pie plate. Trim pastry even with pie plate rim.

3. Roll remaining pastry into a 12-inch-diameter circle. Using a sharp knife, cut slits in pastry. Place pastry circle on filling; trim to ½ inch beyond edge of pie plate. Fold top pastry edge under bottom pastry. Crimp edge as desired. In a small bowl combine egg and the water. Brush pastry with egg mixture; sprinkle with turbinado sugar.

4. Cover edge of pie loosely with foil. Place pie on center oven rack. Line a baking sheet with foil; place on bottom rack to catch any drips. Bake 30 minutes (50 minutes for frozen berries). Remove foil from pie. Bake 35 to 40 minutes more or until pastry is golden and filling is bubbly. If pastry begins to brown too quickly, cover top of pie loosely with foil. Cool on a wire rack.

TRIPLE-BERRY PIE

5. For topping, in a small bowl beat whipping cream with a mixer on medium until soft peaks form (tips curl). Fold in lemon curd. Serve pie with topping. Makes 8 servings.

Pastry for Double-Crust Pie In a large bowl stir together 2½ cups all-purpose flour and 1 teaspoon salt. Using a pastry blender, cut in ½ cup shortening and ¼ cup butter, cut up, until pieces are pea size. Sprinkle 1 tablespoon ice water over part of the flour mixture; toss gently with a fork. Push moistened pastry to side of bowl. Repeat moistening flour mixture, using 1 tablespoon ice water at a time (½ to ⅔ cup total), until flour mixture is moistened. Gather flour mixture into two balls, kneading gently until it holds together.

PER SERVING 527 cal., 25 g fat (11 g sat. fat), 67 mg chol., 402 mg sodium, 71 g carb., 6 g fiber, 30 g sugars, 6 g pro.

As a Gift Spray-paint a pine cone gold; let dry. Place your baked and cooled pie inside a brown pie box and wrap box with twine, raffia, or ribbon. Tie on the pine cone decoration.

NYE
Celebration

Gather friends and ring in the coming year with style and great taste with this selection of appetizers, main dishes, sides, and desserts.

CHOCOLATE
MIXED NUT PIE,
PAGE 143

PICADILLO POPPERS

PICADILLO POPPERS

PREP 45 minutes
GRILL 8 minutes

8   oz. lean ground beef
⅓   cup chopped onion
1   8.8-oz. pouch cooked Spanish-
     style rice
1   cup shredded Monterey Jack
     cheese
½   cup golden raisins
½   cup sliced pimiento-stuffed green
     olives
1   to 2 Tbsp. dry sherry or lime juice
24   plump jalapeño peppers*

1. For filling, in a large skillet cook ground beef and onion over medium-high heat until meat is browned and onion is tender. Drain off fat. Stir in the next five ingredients (through sherry).
2. Cut a lengthwise slit in one side of each jalapeño to create a pocket (do not cut pepper in half). Cut a small crosswise slit on both ends of the long slit, making an I-shape opening. Leave stem intact and use a small spoon to remove seeds and membrane. Spoon filling into peppers.
3. Place filled peppers, slit sides up, in a greased grill basket or grilling pan. Grill, covered, over medium heat 8 to 12 minutes or until peppers are crisp-

tender and filling is heated through. If desired, top peppers with additional cheese. Makes 24 servings.
PER SERVING *74 cal., 4 g fat (2 g sat. fat), 11 mg chol., 107 mg sodium, 7 g carb., 1 g fiber, 3 g sugars, 4 g pro.*
*Tip Chile peppers contain oils that can irritate your skin and eyes. Wear plastic or rubber gloves when working with them.

PARMESAN-STUFFED DATES

PREP 20 minutes
BAKE 12 minutes at 400°F

12   fresh Medjool dates (about 12 oz.)
2   oz. Parmigiano-Reggiano cheese,
     cut into 12 small pieces
6   slices bacon, halved crosswise

1. Preheat oven to 400°F. Using a sharp knife, cut a slit in each date and remove the pit. Stuff each date with a piece of cheese. Wrap each with a bacon half and secure with a toothpick. Place stuffed dates in a 13×9-inch baking pan.
2. Bake 12 to 14 minutes or until bacon is crisp. Serve warm. Makes 12 servings.
PER SERVING *172 cal., 10 g fat (4 g sat. fat), 16 mg chol., 234 mg sodium, 18 g carb., 2 g fiber, 16 g sugars, 4 g pro.*

KALE DIP

PREP 20 minutes
CHILL 1 hour

1   6-oz. carton plain Greek yogurt
½   cup mayonnaise
1   cup finely chopped kale
½   cup chopped cucumber
1   Tbsp. snipped fresh dill
2   tsp. lemon juice
     Salt and black pepper
     Fresh dill weed sprigs (optional)
     Toasted pita chips and/or cut-up
     vegetables

1. In a medium bowl stir together the first six ingredients (through lemon juice). Season to taste with salt and pepper. Cover and chill 1 hour or up to 3 hours.
2. Stir before serving. If desired, top dip with fresh dill sprigs. Serve with chips and/or vegetables. Makes 16 servings.
PER SERVING *60 cal., 6 g fat (1 g sat. fat), 4 mg chol., 67 mg sodium, 1 g carb., 0 g fiber, 1 g sugars, 1 g pro.*

KALE DIP

GOLDEN WASSAIL

ROASTED SALMON WITH HERBS AND YOGURT

CHAMPAGNE PARTY PUNCH

START TO FINISH 10 minutes

- 2   750-ml. bottles Champagne, chilled
- 1   750-ml. bottle Moscato, chilled
- 4   cups sparkling water, chilled
- 1½   cups Cognac
       Kumquats (optional)

1. In a punch bowl stir together Champagne, Moscato, sparkling water, and Cognac. If desired, garnish with kumquats on skewers. Makes 15 servings.
PER SERVING *206 cal., 0 fat, 0 mg chol., 14 mg sodium, 12 g carb., 3 g fiber, 5 g sugars, 1 g pro.*

GOLDEN WASSAIL

START TO FINISH 25 minutes

- 4   cups unsweetened pineapple juice
- 4   cups apple cider or apple juice
- 1½   cups apricot nectar
- 1   cup orange juice
- 2   3-inch sticks cinnamon
- 1   tsp. whole cloves
- ¼   tsp. cardamom seeds, crushed
       Apple slices (optional)
       Fresh bay leaves (optional)

1. In a large saucepan combine all ingredients. Bring to boiling; reduce heat. Simmer, uncovered, 15 minutes. Strain; discard cloves and cardamom. Transfer punch to bowl. If desired, garnish with additional cinnamon sticks, apple slices, and fresh bay leaves. Makes 10 servings.
Tip If desired, moisten the edge of the punch bowl with water or juice. Spread gold decorating sugar in a large shallow dish. Dip the edge of the punch bowl in the sugar to coat.
PER SERVING *133 cal., 0 g fat, 0 mg chol., 13 mg sodium, 32 g carb., 0 g fiber, 28 g sugars, 1 g pro.*

ROASTED SALMON WITH HERBS AND YOGURT

PREP 20 minutes
ROAST 25 minutes at 325°F

- 1   2½-lb. fresh salmon fillet
       Sea salt and freshly ground black pepper
- 1   Tbsp. olive oil
- 2   tsp. dried oregano, crushed
- 1   lemon
- 1   cup plain Greek yogurt
- 1½   cups finely chopped English cucumber
- 3   Tbsp. finely chopped shallots
- 2   Tbsp. snipped fresh Italian parsley
- 2   Tbsp. snipped fresh mint
- 2   Tbsp. snipped fresh dill
- 2   Tbsp. snipped fresh basil
       Dash crushed red pepper

1. Preheat oven to 325°F. Line a shallow baking pan with parchment paper.
2. Rinse salmon; pat dry. Place salmon in prepared baking pan. Sprinkle with salt and black pepper. Drizzle with oil; rub onto salmon. Sprinkle with oregano. Roast 25 to 30 minutes or until salmon flakes easily in center.
3. Remove 1 teaspoon zest from lemon. Cut lemon in half and squeeze juice over salmon. Spoon yogurt onto salmon and top with cucumber, shallots, herbs, crushed red pepper, and lemon zest. Sprinkle with additional salt and drizzle with additional oil. Makes 6 servings.
PER SERVING *328 cal., 15 g fat (3 g sat. fat), 107 mg chol., 195 mg sodium, 5 g carb., 1 g fiber, 3 g sugars, 42 g pro.*

ARGENTINEAN ROLLED FLANK STEAK

Chimichurri In a food processor or blender combine 1¼ cups packed fresh parsley leaves; ¼ cup olive oil; 2 tablespoons coarsely chopped shallot; 2 tablespoons fresh oregano leaves; 2 tablespoons red wine vinegar; 1 tablespoon lemon juice; 4 cloves garlic, coarsely chopped; ½ teaspoon salt; and ½ teaspoon crushed red pepper. Cover and process or blend until nearly smooth.

PER SERVING *631 cal., 28 g fat (7 g sat. fat), 61 mg chol., 1,273 mg sodium, 58 g carb., 1 g fiber, 2 g sugars, 36 g pro.*

*Tip If desired, wrap tortillas in foil and place on the side of grill rack 10 minutes or until warm, turning once.

CARAMELIZED ONION FLATBREAD

PREP 20 minutes
COOK 20 minutes
BAKE 10 minutes at 475°F

¼	cup olive oil
2	large onions, thinly sliced
4	tsp. granulated sugar or packed brown sugar
1	1-lb. portion frozen pizza dough, thawed, or one 1-lb. portion fresh pizza dough
1	14.5-oz. can diced tomatoes, drained
½	cup finely shredded Parmesan cheese (2 oz.)

1. In a large skillet heat oil over medium heat. Add onions and sugar; stir to coat. Cook about 20 minutes or until onions are browned and caramelized, stirring occasionally. Remove from heat.
2. Preheat oven to 475°F. Lightly grease a large baking sheet. Divide pizza dough in half. On a lightly floured surface, roll out each dough half into a 10×5-inch rectangle. Transfer rectangles to prepared baking sheet, placing them 2 inches apart.
3. Evenly divide caramelized onions and tomatoes between dough rectangles. Sprinkle with Parmesan cheese. Bake 10 to 12 minutes or until crust is golden brown and crisp. Makes 6 servings.

PER SERVING *356 cal., 12 g fat (2 g sat. fat), 6 mg chol., 559 mg sodium, 50 g carb., 3 g fiber, 9 g sugars, 8 g pro.*

ARGENTINEAN ROLLED FLANK STEAK

PREP 40 minutes
GRILL 40 minutes
STAND 10 minutes

1	1¼- to 1½-pound beef flank steak
2	medium Anaheim chile peppers, seeded and chopped (tip, page 132)
½	cup chopped sweet onion
2	cloves garlic, minced
1	Tbsp. vegetable oil
1	Tbsp. snipped fresh oregano
½	tsp. salt
¼	tsp. black pepper
4	oz. sliced cooked Black Forest ham or regular ham
½	cup shredded fontina cheese (2 oz.)
1	recipe Chimichurri
12	6-inch corn tortillas or 7- to 8-inch flour tortillas*

1. Trim fat from meat. Score both sides of meat in a diamond pattern by making shallow diagonal cuts at 1-inch intervals. Place meat between two pieces of plastic wrap. Using the flat side of a meat mallet, pound meat lightly into about a 12×8-inch rectangle. Remove plastic wrap.
2. In a large skillet cook Anaheim peppers, onion, and garlic in hot oil over medium heat 3 minutes or until tender, stirring occasionally. Stir in oregano, salt, and black pepper.
3. Arrange ham slices evenly on meat. Spread ham with pepper mixture; sprinkle with cheese. Starting from a long side, roll up rectangle. Tie in three or four places with heavy 100-percent cotton kitchen string.
4. Prepare grill for indirect medium heat. Place meat on grill rack over drip pan. Cover and grill 40 to 45 minutes or until an instant-read thermometer registers 150°F, turning once halfway through.
5. Remove meat from grill. Cover with foil; let stand 10 minutes. Remove and discard string. Cut meat into 1-inch slices. Serve with Chimichurri and tortillas. Makes 6 servings.

CARAMELIZED
ONION FLATBREAD

BUTTERNUT
SQUASH BISQUE

BUTTERNUT SQUASH BISQUE

PREP 30 minutes
COOK 30 minutes
ROAST 45 minutes at 400°F

Nonstick cooking spray
2½ to 3 lb. butternut squash, halved lengthwise and seeded
¼ cup butter
1 large carrot, coarsely chopped
½ cup coarsely chopped onion
½ cup coarsely chopped celery
2 cloves garlic, minced
2 large Braeburn or Gala apples, peeled, cored, and coarsely chopped
1 32-oz. box reduced-sodium chicken broth
1 cup apple cider or apple juice
1 Tbsp. chopped fresh thyme
½ cup crème fraîche or sour cream
1 recipe Croutons (optional)

1. Preheat oven to 400°F. Coat a large shallow baking pan or a 15×10-inch baking pan with cooking spray. Place squash halves, cut sides down, in the prepared pan. Roast, uncovered, 45 to 60 minutes or until tender. Cool slightly. Scoop out flesh from squash into a bowl (discard skin). You should have 2½ to 3 cups.
2. In a 5- to 6-quart Dutch oven melt butter over medium heat. Add carrot, onion, celery, and garlic. Cook about 10 minutes or until vegetables are tender, stirring frequently. Add roasted squash, apples, broth, cider, and thyme. Bring to boiling; reduce heat. Simmer, covered, about 10 minutes or until apples are tender, stirring occasionally. Remove from heat; cool slightly.
3. When slightly cooled, puree soup in batches in a blender or food processor; return to Dutch oven. Whisk in crème fraîche.
4. Gently reheat over low heat, stirring occasionally and making sure soup does not boil. Remove from heat. Top each serving with Croutons, if desired, and additional fresh thyme. Makes 6 servings.
PER SERVING 213 cal., 11 g fat (7 g sat. fat), 30 mg chol., 655 mg sodium, 26 g carb., 3 g fiber, 11 g sugars, 6 g pro.
Croutons Preheat oven to 250°F. In an extra-large bowl whisk together 1½ sticks

butter, melted; 2 tablespoons garlic salt; 1 tablespoon dried parsley; and ½ teaspoon garlic powder. Whisk well to blend. Add 10 cups cubed day-old or dried bread. Toss to coat. Spread bread cubes in a single layer in a large shallow baking pan. Bake 1 hour, stirring every 15 minutes. Cool completely in pan on a wire rack (croutons will crisp as they cool). Store in an airtight container in the refrigerator up to 3 days or in the freezer up to 3 months.

ICEBERG WEDGE SALAD

START TO FINISH 15 minutes

1 head iceberg lettuce
6 slices bacon, crisp-cooked and halved
3 carrots, thinly bias-sliced
2 green onions, chopped
6 radishes, sliced and/or chopped
¼ cup olive oil
¼ cup red wine vinegar
3 cloves garlic, mashed
¼ tsp. salt
¼ tsp. coarse ground black pepper

1. Trim stem from lettuce while leaving core intact. Cut lettuce in quarters then place wedges on individual serving plates. Arrange bacon, carrots, green onions, and radishes on and around each lettuce wedge.
2. For dressing, in a screw-top jar combine oil, vinegar, garlic, salt, and pepper. Cover and shake until combined. Immediately drizzle over salad. Makes 4 servings.
PER SERVING 232 cal., 19 g fat (4 g sat. fat), 13 mg chol., 473 mg sodium, 10 g carb., 3 g fiber, 5 g sugars, 6 g pro.

ICEBERG WEDGE SALAD

KALE CAESAR
SALAD

ROASTED BEET SALAD WITH
SHREDDED GREENS, GOLDEN
RAISINS, AND PINE NUTS

KALE CAESAR SALAD

PREP 25 minutes
BAKE 25 minutes at 300°F
STAND 30 minutes

8   cloves garlic, peeled
¾   cup olive oil
6   oz. ciabatta bread, cut or torn into
    1-inch pieces (4 cups)
¼   teaspoon salt
6   anchovy fillets, patted dry
¼   cup lemon juice
1   Tbsp. Dijon mustard
2   hard-cooked egg yolks, yolks and
    white separated
    Black pepper
3   bunches Tuscan kale (also called
    dinosaur, black, or Lacinato kale),
    stems removed and leaves sliced
    (18 cups)
⅓   cup freshly grated Parmigiano
    Reggiano

1. Preheat oven to 300°F. For croutons,
mince two of the garlic cloves. In a large
saucepan warm ¼ cup of the oil and the
minced garlic over low heat 5 minutes;
remove. Add bread pieces. Sprinkle with
salt. Stir to coat. Spread bread pieces in a
single layer in a shallow baking pan. Bake

25 minutes or until lightly browned, stirring
once. Cool completely; croutons will
crisp up as they cool. Store in an airtight
container at room temperature up to
24 hours.
2. For dressing, in a blender or small food
processor combine remaining 6 garlic
cloves and ½ cup oil, anchovy fillets,
lemon juice, mustard, and hard-cooked
egg yolks. Cover and blend or process
until smooth. (Or use an immersion
blender.) Season to taste with salt and
pepper. (Dressing can be chilled up to
24 hours; let stand at room temperature
30 minutes before using.)
3. Place kale in an extra-large bowl;
add dressing. Using your hands, work
dressing into kale for 15 seconds. Let
stand 30 minutes or up to 2 hours (or
cover and chill up to 24 hours). To serve
sprinkle salad with cheese and top with
chopped egg whites and croutons.
Makes 12 servings.
PER SERVING *228 cal., 16 g fat (3 g sat. fat),
35 mg chol., 243 mg sodium, 16 g carb.,
2 g fiber, 2 g sugars, 7 g pro.*
Fennel and Pistachio Kale Caesar Salad
Prepare as directed. Top with 1 fennel bulb,
trimmed, cored, and thinly sliced, and
½ cup roasted, salted pistachios, chopped.

ROASTED BEET SALAD WITH SHREDDED GREENS, GOLDEN RAISINS, AND PINE NUTS

PREP 25 minutes
ROAST 55 minutes at 450°F

2   lb. beets with leafy tops
2   sprigs fresh rosemary
3   Tbsp. olive oil
¾   cup balsamic vinegar
    Salt
    Black pepper
1   cup crumbled ricotta salata or feta
    cheese (4 oz.)
⅓   cup golden raisins
2   Tbsp. pine nuts, toasted*

1. Preheat oven to 450°F. Cut tops
from beets; set aside. Place beets and
rosemary on a large piece of heavy foil;
drizzle with 1 tablespoon of the oil. Bring
up two opposite edges of foil; seal with
a double fold. Fold in remaining ends to
completely enclose, leaving space for
steam to build. Roast 55 minutes or until
tender. Carefully open packet to release
steam. Set aside until cool enough to

handle. Peel skins from beets and cut into wedges. Discard rosemary.

2. For balsamic reduction, pour vinegar into a small saucepan. Bring to boiling; reduce heat. Simmer, uncovered, 15 minutes or until reduced to ¼ cup. Cool (reduction will thicken as it cools).

3. Meanwhile, remove stems from beet tops; cut tops into fine shreds. In a large bowl gently toss warm roasted beets and beet tops with remaining 2 tablespoons oil. Season to taste with salt and pepper.

4. Arrange beet mixture on a platter and sprinkle with the remaining ingredients. Drizzle with balsamic reduction. Makes 4 servings.

PER SERVING *343 cal, 19 g fat (5 g sat. fat), 21 mg chol., 602 mg sodium, 36 g carb., 5 g fiber, 26 g sugars, 10 g pro.*

*Tip Toast pine nuts in a dry skillet over medium heat 2 to 3 minutes or just until beginning to turn brown.

ROASTED RADISHES WITH ORANGE VINAIGRETTE

PREP 15 minutes
ROAST 30 minutes at 425°F

1½ lb. radishes, trimmed and halved
3   Tbsp. olive oil
1   orange
1   Tbsp. sherry vinegar or white wine vinegar
1   tsp. honey
     Salt and black pepper

1. Preheat oven to 425°F. Place radishes in a 15×10-inch baking pan. Drizzle with 1 tablespoon of the oil; toss to coat. Roast 30 to 35 minutes or until tender and light brown, stirring once.

2. Meanwhile, remove ½ teaspoon zest and 1 tablespoon juice from orange. For vinaigrette, in a small screw-top jar combine orange zest and juice, vinegar, honey, and remaining 2 tablespoons oil. Cover and shake well. Season to taste with salt and pepper. Drizzle vinaigrette over radishes. Makes 6 servings.

PER SERVING *83 cal, 7 g fat (1 g sat. fat), 0 mg chol., 141 mg sodium, 5 g carb., 2 g fiber, 3 g sugars, 1 g pro.*

ROASTED RADISHES WITH ORANGE VINAIGRETTE

OATMEAL SLICES WITH
DATES AND NUTS

OATMEAL SLICES WITH DATES AND NUTS

PREP 20 minutes
CHILL 1 hour
BAKE 6 minutes per batch at 375°F

1   cup butter, softened
1   cup packed brown sugar
½   cup granulated sugar
1   tsp. baking soda
1   tsp. ground cinnamon
½   tsp. salt
1   egg
1   tsp. vanilla
1¾   cups all-purpose flour
2   cups rolled oats
1   cup pitted dates, chopped
½   cup finely chopped toasted pecans (tip, page 49)

1. In a large bowl beat butter with a mixer on medium to high 30 seconds. Add the next five ingredients (through salt). Beat until combined, scraping bowl as needed. Beat in egg and vanilla. Beat in as much of the flour as you can with the mixer. Stir in any remaining flour, the oats, dates, and pecans.
2. Divide dough in half. Shape each half into a 2-inch-diameter log. Wrap each in plastic wrap or waxed paper; chill dough until firm enough to slice (1 to 2 hours).
3. Preheat oven to 375°F. Use a serrated knife to cut logs into ¼-inch slices; place 2 inches apart on a cookie sheet.
4. Bake 6 to 8 minutes or until edges are light brown. Remove; cool on wire rack. Makes 72 cookies.
PER COOKIES 73 cal., 3 g fat (2 g sat. fat), 9 mg chol., 56 mg sodium, 10 g carb., 1 g fiber, 6 g sugars, 1 g pro.

CHOCOLATE MIXED NUT PIE (PICTURED ON PAGE 130)

PREP 25 minutes
BAKE 45 minutes at 350°F

1   recipe Pastry for Single-Crust Pie
3   eggs, lightly beaten
1   cup light-color corn syrup
⅔   cup packed dark brown sugar
⅓   cup butter, melted
1   tsp. instant espresso coffee powder
1¼   cups dry-roasted salted mixed nuts, coarsely chopped
3   oz. sweet-style Mexican chocolate or bittersweet chocolate, chopped
     Cinnamon ice cream or Cinnamon Whipped Cream (optional)

1. Preheat oven to 350°F. Prepare pastry. On a lightly floured surface, slightly flatten pastry. Roll into a 12-inch circle. Transfer to a 9-inch pie plate, being careful not to stretch pastry. Trim to ½ inch beyond edge of plate, fold under pastry even with rim, and crimp as desired.
2. In a medium bowl whisk together eggs, corn syrup, brown sugar, butter, and espresso powder until combined. Stir in nuts and chocolate.
3. Place pastry-lined pie plate on oven rack. Carefully pour filling into pastry shell. To prevent overbrowning, cover edge of pie with foil. Bake 25 minutes; remove foil. Bake 20 to 25 minutes more or until a knife inserted near center comes out clean. Cool on a wire rack. Cover; chill within 2 hours. If desired, serve with cinnamon ice cream or Cinnamon Whipped Cream. Makes 8 servings.
Pastry for Single-Crust Pie In a medium bowl stir together 1½ cups all-purpose flour and ¼ teaspoon salt. Using a pastry blender, cut in ¼ cup shortening or lard and ¼ cup butter, cut up, until pea size. Sprinkle 1 tablespoon ice water over part of the flour mixture; toss gently with a fork. Push moistened pastry to side of bowl. Repeat moistening flour mixture, gradually adding ice water (¼ to ⅓ cup total) until pastry begins to come together. Gather pastry into a ball, kneading gently just until it holds together.
PER SERVING 717 cal., 42 g fat (18 g sat. fat), 123 mg chol., 319 mg sodium, 82 g carb., 3 g fiber, 58 g sugars, 10 g pro.
Cinnamon Whipped Cream In a small chilled small bowl beat ½ cup heavy cream, 1 tablespoon sugar, 1½ teaspoons coffee liqueur (if desired), ¼ teaspoon vanilla, and ⅛ teaspoon ground cinnamon with a mixer on medium until soft peaks form (tips curl).

UPSIDE-DOWN APPLE HONEY CAKE

PREP 25 minutes
BAKE 35 minutes at 350°F
COOL 35 minutes

1½   cups all-purpose flour
2   tsp. baking powder
¼   tsp. salt
¾   cup milk
½   cup honey
1   tsp. vanilla
½   cup butter, softened
1   cup packed brown sugar

UPSIDE-DOWN APPLE HONEY CAKE

2   medium JonaGold, Crispin, Golden Delicious, Piñata, and/or Pink Lady apples, cored and sliced crosswise into ½-inch rings
½   cup pecan halves
2   eggs, room temperature

1. Preheat oven to 350°F. In a medium bowl stir together the flour, baking powder, and salt. In another bowl whisk together milk, honey, and vanilla.
2. Place ¼ cup of the butter in a 9-inch square baking pan. Place pan in oven until butter is melted. Stir in ½ cup of the brown sugar. Arrange 9 apple slices and the pecan halves in pan.
3. In a large bowl beat the remaining ¼ cup softened butter with a mixer on medium to high 30 seconds. Gradually add the remaining ½ cup brown sugar, beating until light and fluffy. Add eggs; beat 1 minute. Alternately add flour mixture and milk mixture, beating on low after each addition just until combined. Carefully spread batter over apple slices.
4. Bake 35 to 40 minutes or until a toothpick inserted near center comes out clean. Cool in pan on wire rack 5 minutes. Loosen sides of cake; invert onto a plate. Cool 30 minutes; serve warm. Makes 9 servings.
PER SERVING 403 cal., 16 g fat (7 g sat. fat), 70 mg chol., 288 mg sodium, 63 g carb., 2 g fiber, 45 g sugars, 5 g pro.

SPONGE CAKE WITH
BROILED MACADAMIA-
COCONUT TOPPING,
PAGE 154

Casual Fare for Guests

Holiday houseguests add to the fun of the season. Be prepared with delicious recipes perfect for casual, relaxed company meals.

ROASTED CABBAGE WITH PEARS, PAGE 151

MOZZARELLA, PESTO, AND HAM TOASTIES

MOZZARELLA, PESTO, AND HAM TOASTIES

START TO FINISH 45 minutes

1	medium red sweet pepper*
1	shallot, quartered
1	cup toasted whole almonds
1	cup packed fresh mint leaves
1	lemon, zested and juiced
½	cup packed fresh Italian parsley leaves
½	cup extra-virgin olive oil
½	tsp. coarse salt
¼	tsp. freshly ground black pepper
8	slices rustic Italian or sourdough bread
8	oz. fresh mozzarella cheese, sliced
6	oz. thinly sliced black forest ham

1. Preheat oven to 450°F. Place whole pepper on a baking sheet lined with foil. Bake 15 minutes or until charred. Remove; wrap in foil. Let stand 15 minutes. Peel and remove stem and seeds; cut into strips.

2. Meanwhile, for pesto, place shallot and almonds in a food processor; pulse until chopped. Add mint, zest, and parsley; pulse to coarsely chop. Gradually add lemon juice and oil, pulsing after each addition until pesto is coarsely pureed. Season with salt and pepper.

3. Preheat broiler. Toast bread on a baking sheet 4 to 5 inches from heat 1 to 2 minutes. Turn slices; spread half the slices with half the pesto; refrigerate remaining pesto. Top with cheese. Top remaining slices with ham. Broil 2 minutes or until cheese is melted. Top with pepper strips. Assemble sandwiches. Makes 4 servings.

*Or ¾ cup jarred roasted red sweet pepper, cut in strips.

PER SERVING *689 cal., 45 g fat (10 g sat. fat), 59 mg chol., 966 mg sodium, 44 g carb., 8 g fiber, 7 g sugars, 30 g pro.*

BLUE CHEESE- AND WALNUT-STUFFED MUSHROOMS

PREP 20 minutes
BAKE 17 minutes at 425°F

24	large fresh mushrooms, about 2 inches in diameter
½	cup seasoned fine dry bread crumbs
⅓	cup grated Parmesan cheese
⅓	cup sour cream
2	Tbsp. snipped fresh parsley
2	cloves garlic, minced
¼	tsp. black pepper
½	cup crumbled blue cheese (2 oz.)
¼	cup chopped toasted walnuts (tip page 49)
	Nonstick cooking spray

1. Preheat oven to 425°F. Remove stems from mushrooms. Place mushroom caps, stem sides up, in a 15×10-inch baking pan.

2. For filling, in a small bowl combine next six ingredients (through pepper). Stir in blue cheese and walnuts. Spoon filling into mushroom caps. Lightly coat mushrooms with cooking spray.

3. Bake 17 to 20 minutes or until filling is light brown and heated through. If desired top with additional blue cheese and parsley. Makes 24 servings.

PER SERVING *43 cal., 3 g fat (1 g sat. fat), 5 mg chol., 103 mg sodium, 3 g carb., 0 g fiber, 0 g sugars, 2 g pro.*

Bacon- and Cheddar-Stuffed Mushrooms Prepare as directed, except omit blue cheese and walnuts. Stir ½ cup shredded cheddar cheese (2 oz.) and 4 slices bacon, crisp-cooked and crumbled, into filling.

BLUE CHEESE- AND
WALNUT-STUFFED
MUSHROOMS

SAUSAGE AND SPINACH SKILLET PIZZA

PREP 35 minutes
BAKE 15 minutes at 475°F
STAND 7 minutes

1   15-oz. can tomato sauce
3   Tbsp. grated Parmesan cheese
2   Tbsp. tomato paste
¾   tsp. dried oregano, crushed
½   tsp. dried basil, crushed
⅛   tsp. crushed red pepper
1   5- to 6-oz. pkg. fresh baby spinach
2   tsp. water
     Olive oil
1   lb. frozen pizza or bread dough, thawed
8   oz. bulk Italian sausage, cooked and drained
1½ to 2 cups shredded mozzarella cheese
     Crushed red pepper (optional)

1. Preheat oven to 475°F. In a small bowl combine tomato sauce, 2 tablespoons of the Parmesan cheese, the tomato paste, oregano, basil, and the ⅛ teaspoon crushed red pepper. Set aside.
2. Place spinach in a large microwave-safe bowl; sprinkle with the 2 teaspoons water. Cover with a microwave-safe plate. Heat on high f 30 seconds. Continue cooking in 10-second intervals just until spinach is wilted. Let stand 2 minutes; carefully remove plate. Transfer spinach to a sieve; press out excess liquid.
3. Brush a 12-inch cast-iron or other heavy oven-going skillet with oil. On a lightly floured surface, roll pizza dough into a 14-inch circle. Transfer to the prepared skillet. Roll edges to form a rim. Brush dough lightly with oil. Spread tomato sauce mixture on dough; top with sausage and spinach. Sprinkle with mozzarella cheese and the remaining Parmesan cheese.
4. Cook pizza in skillet over medium-high heat 3 minutes. Place skillet in oven. Bake 15 to 20 minutes or until crust and cheeses are lightly browned. Let stand 5 minutes before serving. Using a spatula, slide pizza out of skillet. Cut into wedges. If desired, sprinkle with additional crushed red pepper. Makes 6 servings.
PER SERVING *449 cal., 23 g fat (9 g sat. fat), 53 mg chol., 1,237 mg sodium, 40 g carb., 3 g fiber, 5 g sugars, 19 g pro.*

FATTOUSH SALAD

START TO FINISH 25 minutes

2   Tbsp. vegetable oil
2   pita bread rounds, torn into bite-size pieces
¼   cup olive oil
¼   cup lemon juice
2   cloves garlic, minced
½   tsp. ground sumac (optional)
¼   tsp. kosher salt
¼   tsp. freshly ground black pepper
4   cups torn romaine lettuce
½   medium cucumber, seeded and coarsely chopped
½   cup sliced radishes
½   cup sliced green onions
¼   cup chopped fresh mint and/or parsley
½   cup crumbled ricotta salata cheese

1. In a large skillet heat 1 tablespoon vegetable oil over medium-high heat. Add half the pita pieces. Cook 2 to 3 minutes or until toasted, stirring occasionally. Transfer pita pieces to paper towels to drain. Repeat with remaining oil and pita pieces.
2. For dressing, in an extra-large bowl whisk together the next six ingredients (through pepper).
3. Add the next five ingredients (through mint) to dressing in bowl; toss to coat. Add pita pieces and cheese; toss to mix. Makes 4 servings.
PER SERVING *331 cal., 24 g fat (5 g sat. fat), 13 mg chol., 486 mg sodium, 24 g carb., 3 g fiber, 3 g sugars, 6 g pro.*
Tip To bake pita pieces, preheat oven to 350°F. Omit vegetable oil. Lightly coat torn pita bread with nonstick cooking spray. Arrange pita pieces in an even layer in a 15×10-inch baking pan. Bake 10 to 15 minutes or until golden and crisp.

SAUSAGE AND
SPINACH SKILLET
PIZZA

HONEY-GLAZED
PORK AND FENNEL

HONEY-GLAZED PORK AND FENNEL

PREP 15 minutes
ROAST 30 minutes at 425°F
REST 5 minutes

1½ to 1¾ lb. pork tenderloin
    Coarse salt and freshly ground
    black pepper
⅓   cup cider vinegar
⅓   cup honey
1   Tbsp. Dijon mustard
4   cloves garlic, coarsely chopped
2   Tbsp. olive oil
2   medium fennel bulbs, trimmed and
    cut into ¾-inch wedges (fronds
    reserved)

1. Preheat oven to 425°F. Line a 15×10-inch baking pan or small roasting pan with foil. Place pork in pan; season with salt and black pepper on all sides. For glaze, in a small bowl whisk together vinegar, honey, mustard, and garlic. While whisking, slowly add olive oil. Chop reserved fennel fronds (up to ½ cup); stir into glaze.
2. Pour glaze over pork. Add fennel wedges to pan; toss in glaze that collects in the pan until wedges are coated. Roast 30 to 35 minutes or until pork is done (145°F). Cover with foil. Let rest 5 minutes before slicing. Top with microgreens or fresh herbs. Makes 4 servings.
PER SERVING *356 cal., 8 g fat (2 g sat. fat), 111 mg chol., 310 mg sodium, 33 g carb., 4 g fiber, 28 g sugars, 37 g pro.*

ROASTED CABBAGE WITH PEARS

ROASTED CABBAGE WITH PEARS

PREP 15 minutes
ROAST 35 minutes at 425°F

1   1½-lb. head savoy, green, or
    red cabbage, trimmed and cut
    into 8 wedges
    Olive oil
    Salt
    Black pepper
3   Bosc, Anjou, or Bartlett pears,
    halved lengthwise and cored
2   Tbsp. fresh lemon juice
¾   cup chopped walnuts, toasted (tip,
    page 49)
½   cup crumbled blue cheese

1. Preheat oven to 425°F. Place cabbage in a 15×10-inch baking pan. Drizzle with oil and sprinkle with salt and pepper.
2. Roast 35 to 40 minutes or until tender, turning cabbage once and adding pears the last 10 to 15 minutes of roasting time.
3. Drizzle lemon juice over cabbage mixture. Sprinkle with walnuts and cheese. Makes 4 servings.
PER SERVING *364 cal., 25 g fat (5 g sat. fat), 11 mg chol., 529 mg sodium, 32 g carb., 10 g fiber, 16 g sugars, 10 g pro.*

ROOT VEGETABLE
AND POMEGRANATE
COUSCOUS

CHIMICHURRI-TOSSED MUSHROOMS WITH HAZELNUTS

PREP 20 minutes
CHILL 2 hours

¼ cup packed fresh cilantro leaves
¼ cup packed fresh parsley leaves
1 Tbsp. fresh oregano leaves
2 cloves garlic, peeled
½ tsp. kosher salt
⅔ cup extra-virgin olive oil
1½ Tbsp. sherry vinegar or red wine vinegar
1 tsp. Asian chile paste (sambal oelek) or other chile garlic paste
8 oz. large white button mushrooms, sliced ¼-inch thick
⅓ cup hazelnuts, toasted (tip, page 101)
Toasted quinoa*

1. In a food processor combine cilantro, parsley, oregano, garlic, and salt. Cover and pulse until finely chopped. Add ⅔ cup olive oil and pulse 5 seconds. Pour oil mixture into a medium bowl and stir in vinegar and chile paste. Add sliced mushrooms; toss to combine. Transfer mushrooms to a large platter.
2. Cover and chill 2 hours or up to 24 hours before serving. Top with hazelnuts and toasted quinoa. Sprinkle with additional fresh parsley leaves. Makes 6 servings.
*Toasted Quinoa Rinse 3 to 4 tablespoons of uncooked quinoa; drain. Heat a large skillet over medium heat. Add quinoa. Cook and stir 5 minutes or until toasted.
PER SERVING 290 cal, 29 g fat (4 g sat. fat), 0 mg chol., 187 mg sodium, 6 g carb., 2 g fiber, 1 g sugars, 3 g pro.

ROOT VEGETABLE AND POMEGRANATE COUSCOUS

PREP 30 minutes
ROAST 25 minutes at 425°F

1½ tsp. coarse salt
½ tsp. ground cumin
½ tsp. ground cinnamon
¼ tsp. ground ginger
¼ tsp. freshly ground black pepper
2 lb. root vegetables, such as carrots, parsnips, turnips, and/or winter squash, peeled and chopped or sliced ½ inch thick
1 large red onion, cut into 1-inch wedges
2 Tbsp. olive oil
1 cup couscous
1 cup boiling water
½ cup roasted whole almonds, coarsely chopped
½ cup pomegranate seeds

Fresh mint or cilantro sprigs (optional)
Orange wedges (optional)

1. Preheat oven to 425°F. In a large heatproof bowl combine 1 teaspoon of the salt, the cumin, cinnamon, ginger, and pepper. Add root vegetables and onion. Drizzle with oil; toss to coat. Spread in a single layer in two shallow baking pans. Roast 25 to 30 minutes or until tender, stirring once.
2. Meanwhile, in same bowl stir together couscous, the boiling water, and remaining ½ teaspoon salt. Cover tightly with plastic wrap or a lid and let stand 5 minutes. Fluff with a fork.
3. Serve vegetables with couscous. Top with almonds, pomegranate seeds, and if desired, mint. If desired, serve with orange wedges. Makes 4 servings.
PER SERVING 492 cal, 17 g fat (2 g sat. fat), 0 mg chol., 514 mg sodium, 77 g carb., 13 g fiber, 16 g sugars, 13 g pro.

CHIMICHURRI-
TOSSED MUSHROOMS
WITH HAZELNUTS

SPONGE CAKE WITH BROILED MACADAMIA-COCONUT TOPPING

PREP 15 minutes
BAKE 25 minutes at 350°F
COOL 10 minutes
BROIL 2 minutes

1   cup all-purpose flour
1   tsp. baking powder
2   eggs, room temperature
½   tsp. vanilla
1   cup granulated sugar
½   cup milk
2   Tbsp. butter
1   recipe Broiled Macadamia-Coconut Topping

1. Preheat oven to 350°F. Grease a 9-inch square baking pan. Combine flour and baking powder.
2. In a large bowl beat eggs and vanilla with a mixer on high 4 minutes or until thick and lemon-color. Gradually add sugar, beating on medium 5 minutes or until sugar is almost dissolved. Gradually add the flour mixture, beating on low to medium just until combined. In a small saucepan heat milk and butter over low heat until the butter melts. Add milk mixture to egg mixture, stirring just until combined. Pour batter into prepared pan.
3. Bake 25 to 30 minutes or until top springs back when lightly touched. Cool in pan 10 minutes. Carefully spread Broiled Macadamia-Coconut Topping over warm cake. Broil about 4 inches from heat 2 to 3 minutes or until lightly browned and bubbly. Cool in pan on wire rack. Makes 9 servings.

Broiled Macadamia-Coconut Topping
In a medium bowl combine 1 cup flaked coconut; ½ cup packed brown sugar; ½ cup macadamia nuts or slivered almonds, chopped; ¼ cup butter; and 2 tablespoons milk.

PER SERVING *368 cal., 17 g fat (9 g sat. fat), 63 mg chol., 192 mg sodium, 51 g carb., 2 g fiber, 39 g sugars, 4 g pro.*

SPONGE CAKE WITH BROILED MACADAMIA-COCONUT TOPPING

DULCE DE LECHE-MARSHMALLOW BROWNIES

PREP 30 minutes
BAKE 20 minutes at 350°F

1   cup butter
6   oz. unsweetened chocolate, coarsely chopped
2   cups sugar
4   eggs
2   tsp. vanilla
1⅓   cups all-purpose flour
½   tsp. baking soda
1   cup miniature semisweet chocolate pieces
1   13.4-oz. can dulce de leche
1   7-oz. jar marshmallow creme
½   cup chopped pecans, toasted (tip, page 49)

1. In a medium saucepan heat and stir butter and unsweetened chocolate over low heat until melted and smooth. Set aside to cool.
2. Preheat oven to 350°F. Line a 13×9-inch baking pan with foil, extending foil over edges of pan. Grease foil.
3. Stir sugar into cooled chocolate mixture. Add eggs, one at a time, beating with a wooden spoon after each addition just until combined. Stir in vanilla. In a small bowl stir together flour and baking soda. Add flour mixture to chocolate mixture; stir just until combined. Stir in semisweet chocolate pieces. Spread batter in prepared baking pan.
4. Bake 20 to 25 minutes or until edges are set and center is almost set. Meanwhile, transfer dulce de leche to a small microwave-safe bowl. Microwave on high 1 minute or until softened, stirring once. Place pan on wire rack. Immediately spoon mounds of marshmallow creme on hot brownies. Drop spoonfuls of dulce de leche between mounds of marshmallow creme. Let stand a few minutes to soften. Use a knife or thin metal spatula to swirl marshmallow creme and dulce de leche together. Sprinkle with chopped pecans. Cool on a wire rack.
5. Using the edges of foil, lift uncut brownies out of pan. Cut into bars. Refrigerate leftover brownies in an airtight container up to 3 days. Makes 32 brownies.

PER BROWNIE *264 cal., 13 g fat (8 g sat. fat), 45 mg chol., 91 mg sodium, 35 g carb., 1 g fiber, 26 g sugars, 4 g pro.*

DULCE DE LECHE-
MARSHMALLOW
BROWNIES

Index